THIS BOOK BELONGS TO

2020
CHRISTMAS
WITH
Southern Living
INSPIRED IDEAS FOR HOLIDAY COOKING
AND DECORATING

Southern Living BOOKS

MERRY CHRISTMAS!

Every year we are excited to share the newest edition of this book, and 2020 is no different. Whether you have enjoyed every volume since this series was first published or this is the very first time you are holding a copy, we hope you find joy and inspiration as you flip through these pages, peruse the mouthwatering recipes perfected in our Test Kitchen, and begin to visualize your plan for the upcoming holiday season.

In the South, we take pride in our treasured traditions and value our family heirlooms whether it's monogrammed silver, fine china, a vintage tree topper, or cherished hand-knit stockings. Likewise, for almost four decades *Christmas with Southern Living* has been lovingly collected volume by volume. These collections have been shared, passed down, dog-eared, and kitchen-splattered. We hope you will continue this timeless tradition and share it with those coming up in your family—the daughters, nieces, cousins, and godchildren. Don't forget the brides, new homeowners, and graduates too. Send a book or share the series, but help us keep the tradition going strong for a generation of new readers, decorators, cooks, and planners.

Instead of over the river and through the woods, in this edition we explore Christmas All Through the House by sharing inspired ways to decorate for the holidays starting at the mailbox, stepping through the garden gate, stopping on the porch for a spell before exploring a home's-worth of approachable decorating ideas that you can easily re-create. Of course, there are menus for every occasion the season serves up, as well as a cookbook packed with the sweet and savory, the simple and sublime, and always the celebratory recipes you've come to count on from *Southern Living*.

Cheers!

Katherine Cobbs

Katherine Cobbs
Editor

CONTENTS

DECORATE

HOLIDAY LOOKBOOK

CHRISTMAS ALL THROUGH THE HOUSE

Welcome them home with lots of Christmas cheer and ample doses of DIY dazzle this year. From mailbox and garden gate to entry and guest room, both natural and handmade elements woven into festive displays are guaranteed to make drivers brake, neighbors stop by for a visit, and your guests smile when they arrive for the many merry gatherings on the holiday horizon.

A white-brick Colonial is a stately canvas for holiday decorating. The garlands, wreaths, swags, and the mailbox decoration took a color cue from the home's green-black shutters and copper lanterns. It's a monochromatic palette that complements the wintry landscape too.

HANGING OF THE GREEN

Woven into garlands and wound into wreaths, evergreen boughs have long been symbols of everlasting life and infinite love used in decorations that mark the beginning of the Advent season. Beyond their characteristic beauty as decorative embellishments, these accents serve as reminders for deeper reflection during the Christmas season. A heavy mixed-evergreen garland gracing the portico roof, columns, and banisters is decidedly more Southern with hundreds of magnolia leaves tucked in. Alternating the glossy leaf fronts with copper-colored velvety leaf backs provides striking contrast that draws the eye. Olive branches—symbols of peace—add lacy texture and a touch of silver to the abundant mix.

Deck the Outdoors

Letters to Santa (opposite) There is a long-standing tradition in the South of decorating roadside mailboxes. Whether you keep it simple or take it over-the-top, let the curb appeal start here. Save cuttings from the bottom of your Christmas tree to use in your decorating schemes. Evergreen boughs, berries, fruit, and pinecones wired to a well-soaked floral foam form and tied with a bow are all it takes to say "Christmas is here!"

Window Dressing (page 15) Don't let the first cold snap leave your windowboxes bare. Plant miniature cold-hardy shrubs in early fall and fill in the base with reindeer moss and a few festive accents like these metallic stars. Tuck in a bit of the greenery used in the garlands and wreaths for continuity.

Light the Way (at left) Dress up lanterns, lampposts, and landscape lighting in holiday style too. An oversized copper lantern on the porch becomes a showstopper filled with shimmering ornaments and a ribbon topper. Christmas lights on trees and homes are classic touches, but consider changing out exterior lantern bulbs for faceted ones, which disperse light for added twinkle.

A WINTER WELCOME

The fire is lit,
the stockings are hung,
the halls are decked,
the time for family has come.

An inviting holiday interior starts just inside the front door. Give rooms
off of the entryway extra attention since that's what they'll get when guests
arrive. There is no need to decorate every nook and cranny. Choose one
focal point, such as a mantel or sideboard, and make it the
jaw-dropping spotlight of the room.

Repeating Elements

Outside In Make your indoor decor an extension of what graces your home's exterior for consistency and to keep your decorating game plan easy. Inside, twinkle lights intertwined with metallic gold garland and spools of pretty ribbon are called into action to take things up a festive notch.

Find Balance Play with symmetry. A magnolia wreath spray-painted in glossy gold is layered over a canvas hung above one side of the mantel to provide visual balance to the trio of stockings dipping below the opposite side. Streams of ribbon hung with frosty ornaments add weight and a whimsical counterpoint to the garland's ends.

Pick a Palette Accents of gold and white woven into a few yards of the same evergreen garland that was used outdoors give the indoor treatment drama and festive sparkle. Ornaments in cream, champagne, and copper and packages wrapped in a mix of patterns in white and gold carry the theme across the room from fireplace to Christmas tree.

Tricks for the Tree There are many tricks to giving a tree wow factor—and it all starts with the lights. It's best to use more than you think you should and connect them according to the instructions on the box to avoid overloads. Tuck strands in close to the tree's trunk as well as near the tips of branches for ethereal dimension. Step back from your efforts from time to time and squint your eyes to find the dark spots that need lighting up. Whether you decorate with heirloom ornaments, homemade creations, or use all-new baubles each season, it helps to mix pieces of varying scale. Fill the gaps between the branches with waves of ribbon or a few well-placed, oversized ornaments, like the giant paper snowflakes used here.

READY TO GATHER

Cue up the Christmas tunes, light the candles, and set the table. Christmas is here and it is time to come together to celebrate and spread good cheer.

Flowers and Fruit

Time to Toast (facing page) The dining room becomes an inviting pass-through for holiday cocktail hour with something special to take in at every turn. For large crowds, turn the dining table into a cocktail station or buffet where guests can fill glasses or plates to enjoy while they mingle.

Poinsettia Magic (above) The colorful, flowerlike bracts of blushing coral poinsettias can be used as cut flowers that last up to two weeks, provided you remove the lower leaves and place the freshly-cut stems in cool water for half an hour. The water will become cloudy as the stems release a milky sap. Change the water regularly until it remains clear.

Tropical Topiary (at left) A wire planter lined with Southern satsumas, a winter-ripening mandarin variety that thrives in the Lower South, and lime green reindeer moss holds a floral foam tree form dense with boxwood clippings. Wooden floral picks secure more citrus used as ornamentation. A bouquet of peach ranunculus is a pretty sidekick.

Festive Formula

Start with a Favorite Color The artwork in this home inspired the splash of turquoise used on the banister garland and the wreaths in the dining room. Shades of orange and gold are a natural color pairing since they sit across from blue and green on the color wheel.

Add Ornamentation Just as a scarf or earrings can make an outfit, a bit of embellishment adds finesse and interest to a decorating scheme. It can be as simple as using a crusty vessel for a centerpiece in a formal setting or wiring sterling silver baby spoons and rattles to a wreath in a nursery. Use what you have and what you love to elevate your creations to fit your style.

Mix Textures Combine shiny and smooth pieces with matte finishes and rough surfaces for added interest. Stick to one or two colors of wrapping paper, but choose rolls with an array of patterns and textures for a cohesive look that is anything but boring.

Surprise and Delight Add something special. A star or angel topping the tree is lovely, but why not a glittery bird with fanciful feathers, a shimmering gold crown, or origami anything? A floral centerpiece on the table is always lovely, but create a conversation piece instead with a citrus topiary, miniature Christmas village beneath a garden cloche, or a tumbleweed wrapped in twinkle lights. Think outside the traditional and forge your own festive path to Christmas wonder.

KITCHEN CONFIDENTIAL

*Don't overlook the busiest gathering place in the house
when it comes to holiday decorating. Let your kitchen set the tone
for the many meals and hours of fellowship to come.*

Go Rustic and Refined

The Secret Sauce (opposite) If you've ever wondered why some homes draw you in and make you want to sit and stay a while, it has everything to do with the details. Punches of red, juicy orange, and lime green make an inviting statement in the room where everyone loves to congregate. It takes just a few minutes to give the kitchen a holiday face lift. Swap out everyday dishes for a few festive pieces. Add greenery, a wreath, and queue up the Christmas playlist because the impression it makes will linger—so will your guests.

Beyond Traditional (at left and above) Fine china and silver have a place, but in the kitchen you can keep things casual. A rough-hewn planter provides a nice contrast to a luscious bouquet of ranunculus, hypericum berries, limelight hydrangeas, pepperberries, and lemon cypress clippings. The hand-forged walnut star provides a striking focal point against a gray backsplash.

A trio of sunset hues, medley of mismatched patterns, and whimsical touches like candy canes, ornaments, and a punched up bouquet in sorbet shades make this a welcoming table for a memorable meal.

Merry and Bright

Oh, What Fun It Is ... (at right) Off the kitchen, a framed collage of pages from expired passports provides an adventurous backdrop for a colorful tree decorated with accents inspired by far-flung locales. A felt garland suggests how much fun a trip someplace might be in the coming year.

Bowl Full of Jelly ... Beans (above) Baking cookies and making candy are enduring holiday rituals, but baking candy bowls out of peppermints takes the pastime to a clever new level. Search for "peppermint bowls" on the Internet to find the easy instructions. The bowls are a fun catchall for an array of colorful candies, but they make sweet parting favors too.

Pull Up a Chair (opposite) No fireplace? No worries. Hang a stocking from every chair at the table and your family and friends won't hesitate to come when called for dinner. Pretty ribbon and double-sided, industrial-strength tape keep the stockings hung behind dining chairs with care.

A butler's pantry-bar that serves as a pass-through gets extra attention. A fun wreath made from wine corks is a fitting touch, and bowls of fruit are easily enlisted into cocktail service. A driftwood tree carries the rustic feel from the kitchen that plays well with shiplap walls and a vase bursting with vibrant, striped amaryllis blooms.

Shine and Shimmer

Fresh and Faux A mix of artificial trees and real deciduous branches offers an array of opportunities to get creative. Use them to hang Christmas greeting cards or holiday invitations, or as a canvas for wow factor. Here, tightly-spaced bands of glimmering ornaments prove that rainbows can trump reindeer this time of year.

PRETTY PAPER

Whether you color outside the lines or can't cut a straight one, consider gift wrapping an opportunity to express your creativity, perfectly personalize a package, or make a unique statement under the tree.

All Wrapped Up and Ready to Show Save that last small slip of gift wrap on the roll to make pretty cutouts for adorning packages. Old tree toppers and garland make great accents tucked beneath satiny ribbon. Knot the ends of ribbons instead of tying the usual bow. Brown paper is an inexpensive, organic backdrop for a wrap of burlap and a boxwood wreath. Craft store tassels and pompoms are fun flourishes.

HEAVENLY PEACE

*Guests appreciate a quiet, comfortable place to rest their heads, but it can
also be a cozy escape from the hustle and bustle of the busy holiday season.
Make it an enchanted space with a canopy of evergreens and string
of shimmering ornaments to conjure starry nights.*

Make It Memorable

Texture and Twinkle (opposite and above right) A lush curtain of evergreen boughs and a swaying mobile of ornaments above a bed layered with pillows lends a dreamlike quality to the guest suite.

The Little Things (above left and at right) A forest of colorful bottle brush trees mingles with ornaments, ribbon, and flickering candles in an eclectic holiday still life on the bedside table. Flowers make any room feel special. Match the blooms to your decor like this bouquet in blush, icy blue, and dusty green.

Hotel comforts like fresh towels, books, a carafe of water, extra reading glasses, and pretty seasonal accents everywhere are special touches for the guest room that make being away feel even better than staying at home.

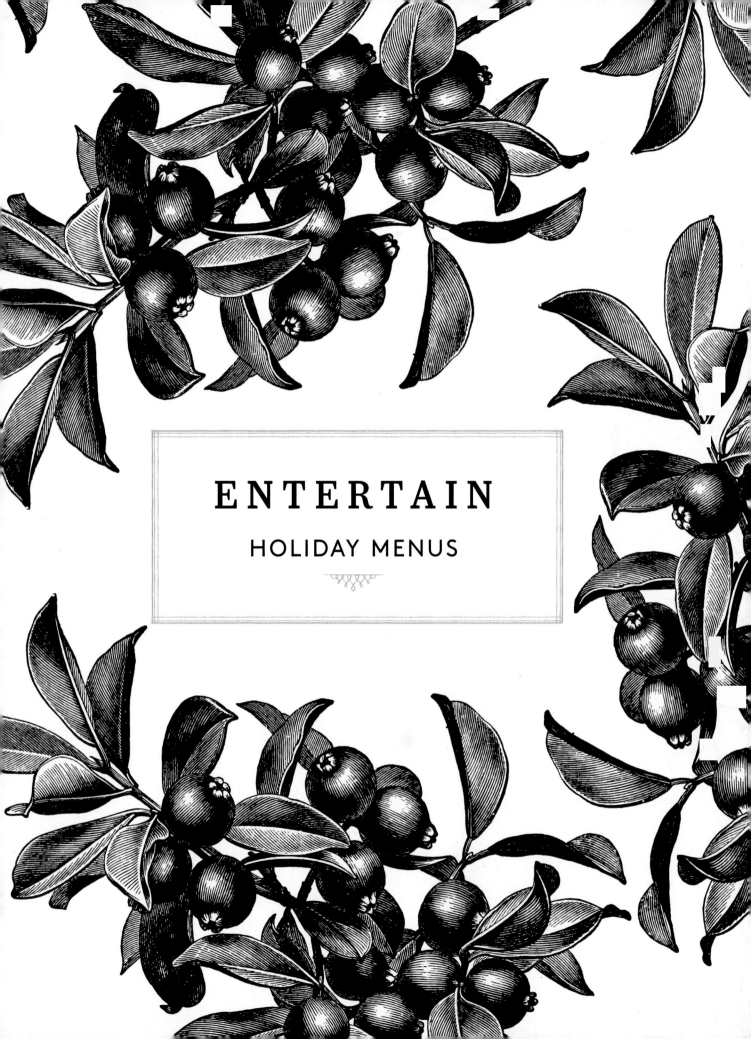

ENTERTAIN

HOLIDAY MENUS

SWEET HOME LUNCHEON

Kick off the season by connecting with friends and family from near and far over a casual lunch that features down-home favorites that everyone comes home craving. These recipes are packed with the regional ingredients and familiar flavors that made them Southern classics.

the menu

SERVES 12

Hibiscus Tea Punch

Bourbon Sweet Tea

Green Chile Cheese Dip

West Indies Cucumber Cups

Greek Salad

AL White Sauce-Smoked Chicken Salad
Tea Sandwiches

Mini BBQ Pork Melts

Peanut Butter-Banana Pudding
Cheesecake Bars

The red seamed roof feels like the holiday bow on top of this traditional Lowcountry cottage. Simple wreaths on every window secured with long loops of shiny red ribbon are all it takes to say "Merry Christmas" and "Welcome, y'all!" A border of white winter annuals adds a bit more pep by the walk, drawing guests along the path to the front door.

Hibiscus Tea Punch

The tart flavor of steeped dried hibiscus blossoms is reminiscent of cranberry—perfectly fitting for the holidays but also deliciously refreshing on hot days in the South. This is one recipe to keep in constant rotation.

MAKES **14 CUPS**   ACTIVE **10 MIN.**
TOTAL **1 HOUR, 20 MIN.**

12 regular-size hibiscus tea bags (such as Celestial
    Seasonings Red Zinger)
6 cups boiling water
³/₄ cup granulated sugar
¹/₂ cup honey
2 (25.4-oz.) bottles sparkling apple-pear juice (such as
    Martinelli's), chilled
Fresh pear slices

1. Place tea bags in a large heatproof pitcher. Pour boiling water over tea bags. Cover; steep 10 minutes. Discard tea bags.

2. Stir sugar and honey into tea until dissolved. Chill at least 1 hour or up to 24 hours.

3. Stir sparkling juice into tea. Pour into ice-filled glasses. Garnish with pear slices.

Tip

To chill big-batch drinks in pitchers and punch bowls without diluting them takes a bit of advance planning. Freeze a portion of the drink in ice cube trays to make ice to float in your serving container to keep the punch cold without affecting its concentration. Or make a double batch of the drink and freeze a portion for ice cubes for the serving glasses. Freeze the rest in a large ice form, Bundt pan, or aspic mold to float in the punch bowl for a pretty presentation. Using frozen fruit is another helpful trick for keeping things chilled.

Hibiscus Tea
Punch

West Indies
Cucumber Cups

Green Chile
Cheese Dip

Bourbon Sweet Tea

This easy punch recipe is great for holiday entertaining and made by adding orange juice and lemonade concentrate to tea infused with cinnamon, fresh ginger slices, and star anise pods. You can prepare this punch up to one day ahead.

SERVES **12** ACTIVE **10 MIN.** TOTAL **1 HOUR, 20 MIN.**

½ cup granulated sugar
4 cups water, divided
2 family-size black tea bags
4 whole star anise
1 (3-in.) cinnamon stick
1 (1-in.) piece fresh ginger, peeled and sliced
2 cups (16 oz.) bourbon
1 cup refrigerated orange juice
½ cup frozen lemonade concentrate (from 1 [12-oz.] can), thawed and undiluted
Lemon and orange slices
Mint sprigs, optional

1. Bring sugar and 2 cups of the water to a boil in a heavy saucepan over high. Cook, stirring occasionally, until sugar dissolves, about 3 minutes; remove from heat. Add tea bags, star anise, cinnamon, and ginger; steep, uncovered, 10 minutes.

2. Pour mixture through a fine-mesh strainer into a large pitcher; discard solids. Add bourbon, orange juice, lemonade concentrate, and remaining 2 cups water; stir well. Chill at least 1 hour or up to 1 day.

3. To serve, pour into ice-filled glasses; garnish with lemon and orange slices and, if desired, mint sprigs.

Green Chile Cheese Dip

A trio of white cheeses—ricotta, sharp white Cheddar, and pepper Jack—adds complex cheesy goodness to this snowy spin on pimiento cheese. Be sure to grate the cheese yourself for the best results. Chopped green chiles stand in for the usual pimientos, adding lots of zesty flavor and a festive pop of green to this white cheese dip.

MAKES **3¾ CUPS** ACTIVE **15 MIN.** TOTAL **15 MIN.**

8 oz. pepper Jack cheese, shredded (about 2 cups)
8 oz. sharp white Cheddar cheese, shredded (about 2 cups)
¾ cup whole-milk ricotta cheese
¼ cup mayonnaise
2 ½ Tbsp. drained canned chopped green chiles
½ tsp. black pepper
¼ tsp. table salt
¼ tsp. garlic powder
¼ tsp. cayenne pepper
¼ cup sliced green onions
Red pepper flakes, sliced green onions, chopped fresh cilantro
Raw vegetables and crackers for serving

Stir together first 10 ingredients in a bowl. Store in an airtight container in refrigerator up to 3 days. Sprinkle with red pepper flakes, sliced green onions, and chopped fresh cilantro to serve.

Tasty Traditions

Pimiento cheese is the pâté of the South. Many consider it the best thing to happen to the sandwich since sliced bread. Spelled pimiento or pimento (both correct), this cheese concoction is as essential to our Southern identity as sweet tea. Dress it up or down, but be sure to use freshly shredded cheese. The pre-shredded stuff is tossed with an anti-caking agent that has no place here.

Below is another tasty spin on white pimiento cheese, accented with red and green, so it seems tailor-made for holiday entertaining.

Holiday Pimiento Cheese: Stir together ½ cup mayonnaise; 3 (4-oz.) jars diced pimiento, drained; ¼ cup sliced green onions; 1 Tbsp. dry mustard; 1 ½ Tbsp. Worcestershire sauce; 1 ½ tsp. hot sauce; ¾ tsp. celery seeds; ¾ tsp. apple cider vinegar; ¼ tsp. salt; and ¼ tsp. black pepper. Stir in 5 cups freshly grated white Cheddar cheese (1 ¼ lb.) until well blended. Cover and chill 8 to 24 hours. Garnish with sliced green onions, if desired. Makes about 5 cups.

West Indies Cucumber Cups

This classic seafood salad with Mobile Bay roots is always a crowd-pleaser. Spooning it into crisp cucumber cups makes it an elegant two-bite appetizer.

SERVES **10**   ACTIVE **30 MIN.**   TOTAL **2 HOURS, 30 MIN.**

1 lb. fresh claw crabmeat, drained and picked over
1 cup finely chopped sweet onion (from 1 large onion)
¼ cup apple cider vinegar
¼ cup canola oil
¼ cup fresh lemon juice (from 1 lemon)
1 tsp. kosher salt
½ tsp. black pepper
3 English cucumbers, ends trimmed,
    sliced into 30 (1-in.-thick) pieces
3 Tbsp. roughly chopped fresh flat-leaf parsley

1. Gently stir together crabmeat, onion, vinegar, oil, lemon juice, salt, and pepper in a large bowl. Cover and chill at least 2 hours or up to 24 hours.

2. Scoop out seeds from cucumber pieces using a melon baller or small spoon, leaving a thin shell and leaving bottoms intact to form cups. Drain well on paper towels.

3. Stir parsley into crabmeat mixture and spoon about 1 tablespoon mixture into each cucumber cup. (Store any remaining mixture in an airtight container in refrigerator up to 3 days.) Chill prepared cucumber cups until ready to serve or up to 2 hours.

Greek Salad

Festive and colorful, this hearty green salad is a terrific option for entertaining because it offers a little something for everyone. To avoid sogginess, dress the salad no more than 15 minutes before you plan to serve it.

SERVES **8**   ACTIVE **30 MIN.**   TOTAL **30 MIN.**

½ cup olive oil
¼ cup red wine vinegar
1 Tbsp. chopped fresh oregano
3 large garlic cloves, minced (1 Tbsp.)
2 tsp. granulated sugar
1 ½ tsp. black pepper
1 tsp. kosher salt
12 cups torn romaine lettuce (from 1 [24-oz.] pkg.
    lettuce hearts)
2 cups thinly sliced cucumber (from 1 large cucumber)
1 pt. multicolored cherry tomatoes, halved
1 cup vertically sliced red onion (from 1 medium onion)
28 pitted Kalamata olives, halved (¾ cup)
8 jarred pepperoncini salad peppers, sliced (¾ cup)
2 cups garlic-seasoned croutons
8 oz. feta cheese, broken into large pieces

1. Whisk together oil, vinegar, oregano, garlic, sugar, black pepper, and salt in a small bowl.

2. Toss together lettuce, cucumbers, tomatoes, onion, olives, and salad peppers in a large bowl.

3. Pour dressing over salad; toss to coat. Add croutons and feta; toss gently.

AL White Sauce-Smoked Chicken Salad Tea Sandwiches

Alabama white barbecue sauce turns to mayonnaise rather than the usual tomato sauce as the base. Its creamy tang and peppery bite are a divine complement to smoked chicken. The sauce may be made up to 1 week in advance and stored in an airtight container in the refrigerator.

SERVES **10**   ACTIVE **30 MIN.**   TOTAL **1 HOUR, 30 MIN.**

1 1/2 cups finely chopped smoked chicken or rotisserie chicken
1/4 cup finely chopped scallions (from 2 scallions)
1/4 cup White Barbecue Sauce (recipe follows)
2 Tbsp. chopped dill pickle chips
1 (16-oz.) pkg. firm white sandwich bread (such as Pepperidge Farm)
1/4 cup salted butter, softened
5 butter lettuce leaves (from 1 head), halved

1. Stir together chicken, scallions, barbecue sauce, and chopped pickles in a bowl. Cover and chill at least 1 hour or up to 24 hours.

2. Trim crusts from all bread slices. Spread softened butter evenly on 1 side of each bread slice. Top half of the bread slices with chicken salad (2 to 3 tablespoons per slice). Add 1 lettuce leaf half to each slice, and top with remaining bread slices, buttered sides down. (Reserve any remaining chicken salad and lettuce for another use.)

3. Cut each sandwich into halves; arrange on serving platter. Cover and chill until ready to serve or up to 6 hours.

White Barbecue Sauce

MAKES **ABOUT 2/3 CUP**   ACTIVE **5 MIN.**   TOTAL **5 MIN.**

1/2 cup mayonnaise
1/4 cup apple cider vinegar
1 Tbsp. black pepper
1/2 tsp. granulated sugar
1/8 tsp. table salt
1/8 tsp. cayenne pepper

Whisk together all ingredients in a small bowl. Cover and store in refrigerator up to 1 week.

Mini BBQ Pork Melts

The South's favorite 'cue joint sandwich goes bite-size and gooey. Smoked Cheddar complements the pork while the dill pickle adds a pleasing tart note.

SERVES **10**   ACTIVE **20 MIN.**   TOTAL **30 MIN.**

1/2 (8-oz.) pkg. cream cheese, softened
3 Tbsp. mayonnaise
3 oz. Cheddar cheese, shredded (about 3/4 cup)
10 slider buns
1 lb. smoked pulled pork
10 (3/4-oz.) smoked Cheddar cheese slices
Dill pickle slices, optional

1. Preheat oven to 350°F. Stir together cream cheese and mayonnaise in a bowl until combined; stir in shredded Cheddar. Spread about 1 1/2 teaspoons mixture onto each bun half. Top bottom bun halves evenly with pulled pork and Cheddar slices. Top with top bun halves.

2. Place prepared sandwiches on a baking sheet; cover with aluminum foil. Bake in preheated oven until buns are toasted and cheese has melted, about 10 minutes.

3. If desired, skewer a dill pickle slice to the top of each sandwich with a decorative toothpick. Serve immediately.

Tip

For a grain-free variation, make open-faced "sliders" by using thick slices of cooked sweet potato in place of the bottom slider buns. Top with the pork and cheese and then proceed with Step 2, baking until cheese has melted. Top each with a dill pickle slice to serve.

Peanut Butter-Banana Pudding Cheesecake Bars

If you love banana pudding and cheesecake, this magnificent mash-up is a recipe you'll turn to again and again. The peanut butter flavor here comes from the cookie crust and chopped peanuts. It's very subtle, but oh-so divine.

SERVES **12** ACTIVE **45 MIN.**
TOTAL **10 HOURS, 45 MIN., INCLUDING 8 HOURS CHILLING**

Cooking spray, for greasing baking dish
All-purpose flour, for dusting baking dish
1 ½ cups finely crushed peanut butter
    sandwich cookies (such as Nutter
    Butter) (from 1 [16-oz.] pkg.)
½ cup finely chopped peanuts
¼ cup unsalted butter, melted
2 large ripe bananas, cut into small cubes
1 Tbsp. fresh lemon juice (from 1 lemon)
2 Tbsp. light brown sugar

3 (8-oz.) pkg. cream cheese, softened
1 cup granulated sugar
3 large eggs
2 tsp. vanilla extract
½ cup coarsely chopped peanuts
Optional garnishes: sweetened whipped
    cream, crushed peanut butter
    sandwich cookies, and sliced bananas
    tossed in lemon juice

1. Preheat oven to 350°F. Coat a 9-inch square baking dish with cooking spray; dust with flour. Stir together crushed cookies, finely chopped peanuts, and melted butter in a small bowl until well blended. Press mixture into bottom and up sides of prepared baking dish. Bake in preheated oven 10 minutes. Let cool completely on a wire rack, about 30 minutes. Do not turn oven off.

2. Stir together bananas and lemon juice in a small saucepan; stir in brown sugar. Cook over medium-high, stirring constantly, until sugar dissolves, about 1 minute. Remove from heat.

3. Beat cream cheese with an electric mixer fitted with a paddle attachment on medium speed until smooth, about 3 minutes. Gradually add granulated sugar, beating until blended. Add eggs, 1 at a time, beating until just combined after each addition. Beat in vanilla. Gently stir banana mixture into cream cheese mixture. Pour batter into prepared crust.

4. Bake cheesecake at 350°F until center is almost set, 45 to 55 minutes. Remove from oven; gently run a knife around edge of cheesecake to loosen. Sprinkle cheesecake with coarsely chopped peanuts. Let cool completely on a wire rack, about 1 hour. Cover and chill 8 hours. Cut into 12 bars; top with desired garnishes.

New Orleans' traditions are as rich as roux and as magical as the Crescent City itself. The Christmas season is full of special ones. The Sunday before Christmas, a sea of carolers—locals and visitors alike—gather in the French Quarter for the annual Caroling at Jackson Square, where they raise voices in unison by the flicker of candlelight.

Blushing French Rose 75

This classic Champagne cocktail gets a floral flourish with notes of elderflower and rose from specialty lemonade. Frozen currants are pretty and edible drink chillers that won't dilute the drink as they thaw.

SERVES **10** ACTIVE **5 MIN.** TOTAL **5 MIN.**

1³/₄ cups elderflower-and-rose lemonade (such as Belvoir)
1¹/₄ cups (10 oz.) gin, chilled
3 cups (24 oz.) Champagne or other sparkling wine, chilled
Frozen red currants

1. Stir together lemonade and gin in a pitcher; chill until ready to serve.

2. Just before serving, add Champagne; stir gently. Garnish with frozen berries.

Red Beans-and-Rice Arancini

Emblematic of the Creole classic in miniature, the key to success here is to fry just a few of these at a time. A crowded pan will lower the oil temperature, which will make the arancini greasy. We served these with prepared mayonnaise mixed with Creole seasoning to taste and a squeeze of fresh lemon juice.

SERVES **10** ACTIVE **40 MIN.** TOTAL **7 HOURS**

1 (8-oz.) pkg. red beans and rice mix (such as Zatarain's)
¹/₂ lb. smoked sausage, finely chopped
¹/₄ cup finely chopped scallions (from 3 large scallions)
¹/₂ cup (about 2¹/₈ oz.) all-purpose flour
2 large eggs
¹/₄ cup water
1 cup fine, dry breadcrumbs
Vegetable oil

1. Cook red beans and rice according to package directions, stirring in smoked sausage before cooking. Stir in scallions. Cover and chill at least 4 hours. Shape chilled mixture into 22 balls (about 2 heaping tablespoons per ball).

2. Place flour in a shallow bowl. Whisk together eggs and water in a second bowl. Place breadcrumbs in a third shallow bowl. Dredge red beans-and-rice balls in flour, dip in egg mixture, and roll in breadcrumbs to coat. Place on a parchment paper-lined baking sheet, cover loosely with plastic wrap, and chill at least 30 minutes or up to 24 hours.

3. Pour oil to a depth of 2 inches in a deep saucepan; heat to 350°F. Fry rice balls, in batches, until golden, 2 to 3 minutes per batch. Remove with a slotted spoon; drain on paper towels. Keep warm in a 225°F oven; serve warm.

Rich Black Pepper
Cornbread

Frisée-and-
Raddichio Salad
with Creole Mustard
Vinaigrette

Smoked Turkey, Tasso, and
Mirliton Gumbo

Pompano Rillettes

Pompano en Papillote, which means "in parchment," is a signature baked fish dish at Antoine's in New Orleans. This mild white fish dip is inspired by that classic. It is a savory and elegant change from traditional salmon or smoked trout dip. Try it on your morning bagel for a flavorful protein-packed breakfast.

SERVES **10**   ACTIVE **25 MIN.**   TOTAL **30 MIN.**

³/₄ cup, plus 1 Tbsp. (6½ oz.) unsalted butter, softened, divided
¼ cup plus 2 Tbsp. sour cream or crème fraîche
1 tsp. lemon zest plus 1 Tbsp. fresh juice (from 1 lemon)
2 scallions, finely chopped (about ¼ cup)
1 garlic clove, minced
2 Tbsp. dry white wine
Poached Pompano (recipe follows)
1 Tbsp. chopped fresh flat-leaf parsley
³/₄ tsp. kosher salt
½ tsp. black pepper
Toasted baguette slices

1. Beat ¾ cup of the butter in the bowl of a stand mixer on high speed until soft. Add sour cream, lemon zest, and lemon juice, beating until smooth. Set aside.

2. Melt remaining 1 tablespoon butter in a skillet over medium. Add scallions and garlic; cook, stirring often, until tender, about 2 minutes. Stir in wine, and cook until slightly reduced, about 2 minutes. Remove from heat, and let cool 10 minutes; stir into sour cream mixture until combined.

3. Add Poached Pompano, and beat with an electric mixer on high speed 1 minute. Gently stir in parsley, salt, and pepper; chill until ready to serve. Serve with baguette slices.

Poached Pompano

MAKES **ABOUT ²/₃ CUP**   ACTIVE **10 MIN.**   TOTAL **30 MIN.**

1 cup dry white wine
2 scallions, sliced
1 garlic clove, chopped
¼ tsp. kosher salt
¼ tsp. black pepper
³/₄ lb. skin-on pompano fillets (or red snapper fillets)

1. Bring wine, scallions, garlic, salt, and pepper to a boil in a medium skillet over medium-low.

2. Place pompano, skin-sides down, in poaching liquid. Simmer until fish flakes easily when tested with a fork, 3 to 4 minutes per side.

3. Remove fillets from poaching liquid, and let cool 10 minutes. Using a fork, gently break fish into 1-inch pieces.

Frisée-and-Radicchio Salad with Creole Mustard Vinaigrette

Don't be afraid to combine hearty, bitter greens like frisée and radicchio in salads. Instead, soften their bite with bright, flavorful dressing like this pleasingly acidic vinaigrette. The blue cheese and crispy fried shallots are bold garnishes that complement the greens.

SERVES **10**   ACTIVE **40 MIN.**   TOTAL **40 MIN.**

¹/₃ cup red wine vinegar
1½ Tbsp. Creole mustard
1 tsp. granulated sugar
¼ tsp. kosher salt
¼ tsp. black pepper
³/₄ cup, plus 3 Tbsp. olive oil, divided
2 Tbsp. finely chopped shallot (from 1 shallot)
1½ cups sliced shallots (from 3 shallots)
¼ tsp. kosher salt, divided
2 heads frisée, curly endive, or escarole, torn
1 large head radicchio, torn
1 cup loosely packed fresh flat-leaf parsley, torn
3 oz. blue cheese, crumbled (about ³/₄ cup)

1. Whisk together vinegar, mustard, sugar, salt, and pepper; gradually whisk in ¾ cup of the olive oil. Stir in chopped shallot. Cover and chill until ready to use.

2. Heat 1½ tablespoons of the oil in a medium skillet over medium; add half of the sliced shallots, and cook, stirring often, until lightly browned, about 10 minutes. Remove from skillet, and drain on a paper towel; sprinkle with ⅛ teaspoon of the salt. Repeat procedure with remaining oil, sliced shallots, and salt.

3. Combine frisée, radicchio, and parsley in a large serving bowl; top with blue cheese and fried shallots. Pour dressing over salad, and toss to coat.

Ingredients 101

Frisée (pronounced free-ZAY) is the French term for a type of curly chicory that has pale green, frizzy leaves and a peppery flavor. It is sometimes sold as French chicory or Italian chicory. It is less bitter than other chicories because this variety is blanched in the field about 30 days after planting. Blanching is a process where cultivated plants are covered for a period of time to prevent light photosynthesis and the production of chlorophyll. The vegetable is harvested when it has achieved the optimum pale color and tenderness. Frisée has a more delicate texture and milder flavor than other chicories.

Smoked Turkey, Tasso, and Mirliton Gumbo

A symbol of Creole cooking, gumbo is a Louisiana classic. Tasso ham and filé powder lend flavor and body to this gumbo enriched by a rich, dark roux. Tasso ham can be hard to find outside of Louisiana, so look for it in specialty markets or online. Find smoked turkey thighs in the meat section of your supermarket where you find ham hocks or salt pork. Mirliton is another name for chayote squash, but it is often referred to as a "vegetable pear" in New Orleans, where the beloved squash is served pickled, stuffed with shrimp or crab, deep-fried, or tossed raw in salads.

SERVES **10**   ACTIVE **1 HOUR, 30 MIN.**
TOTAL **2 HOURS, 30 MIN.**

¹/₂ cup vegetable oil
1¹/₄ cups (about 5³/₈ oz.) all-purpose flour
2 cups chopped yellow onion (from 1 large onion)
1 cup chopped green bell pepper (from 1 medium pepper)
1 cup sliced celery (from 2 stalks)
10 cups hot water
1¹/₂ Tbsp. minced garlic (from 5 garlic cloves)
4 bay leaves
1¹/₂ Tbsp. Worcestershire sauce
1 Tbsp. Creole seasoning
1 tsp. hot sauce
³/₄ tsp. dried thyme
4 cups seeded and chopped mirlitons (chayotes)
    (from 2 large mirlitons)
3¹/₂ cups chopped tasso ham (about 1 lb.)
3 cups chopped smoked turkey (from 1 [2-lb.]
    turkey thigh)
1 cup sliced scallions (from 4 large scallions), plus more
    for garnish
Filé powder (optional)
Hot cooked long-grain rice

1. Heat oil in Dutch oven over medium 3 minutes. Whisk in flour, and cook, stirring constantly, until roux is chocolate colored, 25 to 30 minutes.

2. Stir in onion, bell pepper, and celery; cook, stirring often, until tender, about 8 minutes. Gradually stir in hot water, and bring mixture to a boil over high. Add garlic, bay leaves, Worcestershire sauce, Creole seasoning, hot sauce, and thyme. Reduce heat to low, and simmer, stirring occasionally, 1 hour.

3. Stir mirlitons, ham, and turkey into roux mixture; cook 45 minutes. Stir in scallions; cook 30 more minutes. Remove and discard bay leaves.

4. Remove gumbo from heat. Sprinkle with filé powder, if desired. Serve over rice. Sprinkle with scallions.

Rich Black Pepper Cornbread

Greek yogurt is the secret ingredient in this velvety-moist cornbread. It takes the place of the usual buttermilk with the tang you'd expect but a lot more richness. The key to achieving a crisp exterior to contrast with the tender crumb is to get the skillet blistering hot before you add the batter.

SERVES **8**   ACTIVE **15 MIN.**   TOTAL **1 HOUR**

¹/₄ cup bacon drippings, divided
2¹/₂ cups self-rising yellow cornmeal
2¹/₂ cups plain Greek yogurt
¹/₄ cup unsalted butter, melted
2 tsp. granulated sugar
2 tsp. black pepper
2 large eggs

1. Preheat oven to 425°F. Add 2 tablespoons of the bacon drippings to a 12-inch cast-iron skillet; heat in oven 10 minutes.

2. Whisk together cornmeal, yogurt, butter, sugar, pepper, eggs, and remaining bacon drippings; carefully, pour batter into hot skillet.

3. Bake at 425°F until lightly browned, 25 to 30 minutes. Invert onto a wire rack. Cool completely, about 15 minutes.

VARIATION

Cornbread Croutons:

Cut cooled cornbread into 1-inch cubes. Toast at 450°F until golden brown, 5 to 7 minutes.

Tasty Traditions

Southerners have strong opinions about their cornbread. Some say it should only be made with yellow stone-ground cornmeal. Others exclaim that only white cornmeal will do. Folks are equally divided over whether cornbread should be savory or sweet. Our Test Kitchen weighed in too. The cornbread we consider our best includes fine yellow cornmeal, butter, and a touch of sugar. Yes, just a touch! Though we know that just like heated debates over the best way to enjoy okra, fried or stewed, or the origin of Brunswick stew, some arguments will never be settled. One thing we can all agree on: Nothing tastes better than that first bite of piping hot cornbread slathered with butter. The juxtaposition of crusty exterior from a good sear in the cast-iron skillet and the tender crumb inside has made knees buckle for generations of Southerners.

Chestnut Praline Bread Pudding

Say "hello" to your new favorite holiday dessert or Christmas morning breakfast sweet. This recipe hits on all cylinders: the pitch-perfect flavor of nutty pralines, hints of warm holiday spice, and a comforting "chestnuts roasting on the open fire" custard made with canned crème de marrons, which easily can be ordered online if you cannot find it in your local grocery store.

SERVES **12**   ACTIVE **30 MIN.**   TOTAL **3 HOURS**

6 large eggs
2½ cups heavy cream
2½ cups whole milk
½ cup packed light brown sugar
½ cup granulated sugar
¼ cup chestnut cream (crème de marrons)
2 tsp. vanilla extract
¼ tsp. table salt

¼ tsp. ground nutmeg
¼ tsp. ground allspice
1 (16-oz.) day-old French bread loaf, cut into 1-in. cubes (about 14 cups)
1 cup coarsely chopped toasted pecans, plus, if desired, more for garnish
Cooking spray
Praline Sauce (recipe follows)

1. Whisk together eggs, cream, milk, brown sugar, granulated sugar, chestnut cream, vanilla, salt, nutmeg, and allspice in a large bowl. Add bread cubes, stirring to coat thoroughly. Let stand 1 hour, stirring occasionally to ensure an even coating. Stir in pecans.

2. Preheat oven to 350°F. Lightly grease (with cooking spray) a 13- x 9-inch baking dish; pour bread mixture into dish. Bake in preheated oven until bubbly around edges and firm in center, 40 to 45 minutes. Let stand 5 minutes. Sprinkle with chopped pecans, if desired. Serve with Praline Sauce.

Praline Sauce

MAKES **ABOUT 1½ CUPS**   ACTIVE **20 MIN.**   TOTAL **20 MIN.**

3 Tbsp. salted butter
1 Tbsp. all-purpose flour
1 cup heavy cream
½ cup packed dark brown sugar

2 Tbsp. (1 oz.) spiced rum
2 tsp. vanilla extract
¼ tsp. ground nutmeg
⅛ tsp. table salt

Melt butter in a small saucepan over medium-low; whisk in flour, and cook, whisking constantly, until foamy and golden brown, 3 to 4 minutes. Whisk in cream and brown sugar; cook, whisking constantly, until thickened, about 3 minutes. Remove from heat. Whisk in rum, vanilla, nutmeg, and salt. Return to heat, and cook, whisking constantly, until bubbly, 2 to 3 minutes. Use immediately.

BLUEGRASS BRUNCH

Inspired by the authentic flavors and traditional dishes from the rolling hills of Kentucky, this Christmas morning brunch menu is loaded with savory and sweet surprises guaranteed to entice your guests to the table and keep the holiday cheer going right until dinnertime.

the menu

SERVES 8

Bluegrass Mimosas

Grits Fritters with Beer-Cheese Dip

Breakfast Hot Browns with
Henry Bain-Mornay Sauce

Skillet Potatoes

Winter Fruit Salad

Quick Kentucky Modjeskas

Derby Monkey Bread

Rolling hills covered in a dusting of snow turn horse country into a wintry wonderland. It's a captivating scene best enjoyed inside from a warm perch by a roaring fire with family and friends gathered 'round.

Bluegrass Mimosas

A trio of julep staples—sugar, bourbon, and fresh mint—elevates this brunch standard to Triple Crown status.

SERVES **8**   ACTIVE **15 MIN.**   TOTAL **1 HOUR, 20 MIN.**

1 cup sugar
1 cup water
16 large fresh mint leaves
2²/₃ cups refrigerated orange juice
1³/₄ cups sparkling wine or Champagne
1¹/₂ cups club soda
³/₄ cup (6 oz.) bourbon
Orange peel twists

1. Stir together sugar and water in a small saucepan over medium. Bring to a simmer, and cook, stirring occasionally, until sugar is dissolved, about 3 minutes. Remove pan from heat; add mint leaves, and let stand 10 minutes. Remove and discard mint leaves. Cover and chill simple syrup at least 1 hour or up to 24 hours.

2. Stir together chilled simple syrup, orange juice, sparkling wine, club soda, and bourbon in a large pitcher. Garnish with orange twists, and serve immediately.

Grits Fritters with Beer-Cheese Dip

Beer cheese, a Kentucky tavern tradition, becomes a dip for these crispy fritters made from cheese grits and smokehouse bacon.

SERVES **12**   ACTIVE **45 MIN.**   TOTAL **4 HOURS, 45 MIN.**

1 cup whole milk
1 cup water
¹/₂ cup uncooked quick-cooking grits
¹/₂ tsp. kosher salt
3 oz. white Cheddar cheese, shredded (about ³/₄ cup)
¹/₄ cup cooked and finely crumbled bacon (about 4 slices)
1 scallion, minced (about 2 Tbsp.)
¹/₄ tsp. black pepper
Cooking spray
³/₄ cup panko (Japanese-style breadcrumbs)
Vegetable oil
Beer-Cheese Dip (recipe follows)

1. Bring milk and water to a boil in a saucepan over medium-high. Slowly add grits and salt, and reduce heat to medium-low. Cover and cook, stirring occasionally, until thickened, 5 to 7 minutes. Remove pan from heat, and stir in cheese, bacon, scallion, and pepper, stirring until cheese is melted. Spoon mixture into a lightly greased (with cooking spray) 8-inch square baking dish or pan, and spread in an even layer; let stand 10 minutes. Cover and chill at least 4 hours or up to 24 hours.

2. Using a 1¼-inch round cutter, cut grits into rounds. Dredge rounds in panko, shaking off excess.

3. Pour oil to depth of ½ inch in a large, heavy skillet; heat oil over medium-high to 350°F. Fry rounds, in batches, until golden brown and crisp, about 2 minutes on each side. Drain on paper towels. Keep fritters warm on a wire rack in a large pan in a 225°F oven up to 30 minutes. Serve warm with Beer-Cheese Dip.

Make Ahead: Prepare recipe as directed through Step 2, and freeze on a baking sheet 30 minutes or until firm. Transfer to a ziplock plastic freezer bag, and freeze. Cook frozen fritters as directed in Step 3, increasing frying time until golden brown, crisp, and centers are thoroughly heated, about 3 to 4 minutes per side.

Beer-Cheese Dip

MAKES **2 CUPS**   ACTIVE **20 MIN.**   TOTAL **30 MIN.**

¹/₂ (8-oz) pkg. cream cheese, softened
¹/₃ cup amber-colored beer, at room temperature
1 (8-oz.) block extra-sharp white Cheddar cheese, shredded
¹/₂ tsp. hot sauce
¹/₈ tsp. garlic salt

Place cream cheese in a medium saucepan over medium, and cook, whisking often, until melted, about 5 minutes. Gradually add beer, whisking until blended. Gradually add shredded Cheddar, whisking until melted and smooth, 8 to 10 minutes. Stir in hot sauce and garlic salt. Let stand 10 minutes before serving.

Make Ahead: Prepare as directed, cover and chill until ready to serve. Microwave on HIGH until thoroughly heated, about 2 minutes, stirring after 1 minute.

Skillet Potatoes

Winter Fruit Salad

Breakfast Hot Browns with Henry Bain-Mornay Sauce

Breakfast Hot Browns with Henry Bain-Mornay Sauce

The iconic sandwich from The Brown Hotel in Louisville gets the breakfast treatment with a fried egg. Henry Bain Sauce, created by a waiter at Louisville's Pendennis Club, adds a hit of sweetness to traditional mornay sauce.

SERVES **8**   ACTIVE **45 MIN.**   TOTAL **45 MIN.**

8 thick white bread slices (such as Sara Lee Artesano)
Cooking spray
2 tsp. olive oil
8 large eggs
1½ lb. Kentucky ham slices (such as Kentucky Legend)
Henry Bain-Mornay Sauce (recipe follows)
4 plum tomatoes, sliced
16 bacon slices, cooked
8 oz. Parmesan cheese, shredded (about 2 cups)

1. Preheat broiler with oven rack 6 inches from heat. Place bread slices on a baking sheet; broil until toasted, 1 to 2 minutes per side. Arrange bread slices in 8 separate lightly greased (with cooking spray) shallow, broiler-safe baking dishes.

2. Heat a large nonstick skillet over medium. Add olive oil, and swirl to coat. Crack eggs into skillet; cook 2 minutes. Cover and cook until whites are set, about 2 minutes. Remove from heat.

3. Top bread evenly with ham slices. Pour Henry Bain-Mornay Sauce over ham, and top each with 1 fried egg. Top evenly with tomato slices, bacon, and Parmesan cheese. Place baking dishes on baking sheet. Broil until bubbly and lightly browned, about 3 to 4 minutes. Serve immediately.

Note: This may be baked in a single (13- x 9-inch) baking dish instead of individually.

Henry Bain-Mornay Sauce

MAKES **4 CUPS**   ACTIVE **10 MIN.**   TOTAL **10 MIN.**

½ cup (4 oz.) salted butter
⅓ cup (about 1½ oz.) all-purpose flour
3½ cups whole milk
2 oz. Parmesan cheese, shredded (about ½ cup)
¼ cup prepared Henry Bain sauce
1 tsp. kosher salt
¼ tsp. black pepper

Melt butter in a 3-quart saucepan over medium-high. Whisk in flour; cook, whisking constantly, 1 minute. Gradually whisk in milk. Bring to a boil, and cook, whisking constantly until thickened, about 5 minutes. Whisk in Parmesan cheese, Henry Bain sauce, salt, and pepper until blended and smooth. Serve hot.

Skillet Potatoes

Fresh parsley and a grating of lemon zest add freshness to classic pan-fried potatoes. For a change of flavors, substitute another complementary duo like orange zest and rosemary or lime zest and mint instead.

SERVES **8**   ACTIVE **10 MIN.**   TOTAL **30 MIN.**

3 lb. small (about 2 inches in diameter) white or yellow potatoes, halved
3 Tbsp. vegetable oil, divided
4 Tbsp. unsalted butter
2 Tbsp. chopped fresh flat-leaf parsley
1 Tbsp. lemon zest (from 1 lemon)
1½ tsp. kosher salt
½ tsp. black pepper

1. Toss potatoes and 2 tablespoons oil in a microwavable bowl; cover with plastic wrap, and microwave on HIGH until softened, 5 to 7 minutes.

2. Melt butter with remaining 1 tablespoon oil in a large skillet over medium until sizzling. Add potatoes, cut sides down, to skillet, and cook until golden brown on bottom, about 8 minutes. Turn potatoes, and cook until golden brown and tender, about 8 minutes. Transfer potatoes to a large bowl; sprinkle with parsley, lemon zest, salt, and pepper. Toss to coat, and serve hot.

Ingredients 101

Ham is the cured or smoked hind leg of pork. The label on the ham will identify the type of processing. Fully cooked ham does not require heating and can be eaten cold, but it is more flavorful if heated to 140°F. Fresh ham hasn't been cured or smoked and must be cooked to 160°F before serving. Always assume, unless the wrapper indicates otherwise, that a ham needs cooking.

Bone-in ham: whole, butt end, or shank with bone intact

Boneless ham: rolled and packed in netting

Country ham: Prepared with a dry cure, these are salty, and require soaking before cooking. They are referred to by the location or processor where they are produced, such as Smithfield ham, Kentucky ham, or Broadbent's.

Dry-cured ham: rubbed with a mixture of salt, sugar, nitrites, and seasonings, and then air-dried

Fresh ham: uncured, uncooked pork hind leg

Smoked ham: After curing, this is hung in a smokehouse to take on the smoky flavor notes of the wood used.

Winter Fruit Salad

This is a simple yet beautiful platter for any holiday spread. The combination of citrus here is tangy and sweet. Sea salt gives a briny crunch, while arugula and tarragon add a memorable vegetal freshness.

SERVES **8**   ACTIVE **30 MIN.**   TOTAL **40 MIN.**

½ cup honey
½ water
2 tsp. pink peppercorns or red peppercorns
¼ tsp. crushed red pepper
5 cardamom pods, crushed
4 whole cloves
1 (3-inch) cinnamon stick
1 tarragon sprig
3 oranges
3 mandarin oranges
2 Ruby Red grapefruit
2 limes
6 kumquats (optional)
3 cups baby arugula
1 (4.3-oz.) pkg. fresh pomegranate arils
2 Tbsp. fresh tarragon leaves
1 Tbsp. flaky sea salt (such as Maldon)
1 tsp. coarsely crushed pink peppercorns
¼ cup olive oil

1. Bring honey, water, peppercorns, red pepper, crushed cardamom, cloves, cinnamon stick, and tarragon sprig to a boil in a saucepan over medium-high. Boil, stirring often, 1 minute. Remove from heat, and let stand 30 minutes.

2. Meanwhile, peel oranges, grapefruit, limes, and, if desired, kumquats. Cut away bitter white pith from oranges, grapefruit, and limes. Cut fruit crosswise into thin rounds. Arrange fruit and arugula on a serving platter; sprinkle with pomegranate arils.

3. Pour honey mixture through a fine-mesh strainer into a bowl, discarding solids. Drizzle ¾ cup dressing over fruit mixture; reserve remaining dressing for another use (such as flavoring iced tea). Sprinkle top with tarragon leaves, salt, and crushed peppercorns; drizzle with olive oil.

Make Ahead: Prepare as directed; cover and chill for up to 24 hours.

Quick Kentucky Modjeskas

A classic Kentucky confection created in the late 1800s in Louisville in honor of an actress of the same name, Modjeskas are traditionally homemade marshmallows dipped in buttery caramel and served as a solo sweet or with coffee or hot chocolate. We've streamlined the approach by using store-bought marshmallows for ease. Float one on top of coffee or hot cocoa to create a little magic in your mug.

MAKES **ABOUT 5 DOZEN**   ACTIVE **30 MIN.**
TOTAL **1 HOUR, 30 MIN.**

1 (14-oz.) can sweetened condensed milk
1 (11-oz.) pkg. caramel candies
½ cup (4 oz.) salted butter, cubed
1 tsp. kosher salt
1 tsp. vanilla extract
1 (16-oz.) pkg. marshmallows

1. Stir together sweetened condensed milk, caramel candies, and butter in a medium saucepan over low. Cook, stirring often, until butter and caramels are melted and mixture is completely smooth, about 3 minutes. Remove from heat, and stir in salt and vanilla.

2. Using a fork, dip marshmallows in melted caramel mixture, scraping off excess mixture on edges of pan. Place dipped marshmallows on a large wax paper-lined baking sheet. Chill until set, about 1 hour. Store in a single layer in an airtight container in the refrigerator up to 3 days.

Derby Monkey Bread

This sweet morning treat is equally at home on any dessert table. Bourbon, chocolate, and nuts are the ingredients that put "Derby" in the recipe name.

SERVES **10 TO 12**   ACTIVE **30 MIN.**   TOTAL **2 HOURS, 30 MIN.**

1 (25-oz.) pkg. frozen Parker House-style roll dough (such as Bridgford)
Cooking spray
1½ cups granulated sugar
1½ Tbsp. ground cinnamon
¾ cup (6 oz.) salted butter, melted
1 cup miniature semisweet chocolate chips
Bourbon Syrup (recipe follows)
½ cup chopped, toasted pecans

1. Place frozen rolls, 1 inch apart, on a lightly greased (with cooking spray) baking sheet; cover with lightly greased plastic wrap, and let rise in a warm place (80° to 85°F), until dough is thawed and rolls are almost doubled in size, about 1 hour and 15 minutes.

2. Preheat oven to 375°F. Stir together sugar and cinnamon in a medium bowl. Set aside.

3. Cut each thawed roll in half. Dip each half in melted butter, roll lightly in chocolate chips, and then toss in sugar-cinnamon mixture. Arrange rolls in a lightly greased 12-cup Bundt pan, overlapping slightly. Bake in preheated oven until golden brown, about 30 minutes. Cool in pan 5 minutes; invert bread onto a wire rack, and cool 15 minutes.

4. Drizzle top of warm bread with 3 to 4 tablespoons Bourbon Syrup. Sprinkle pecans over bread. Drizzle with remaining Bourbon Syrup.

Bourbon Syrup

MAKES ½ **CUP**   ACTIVE **5 MIN.**   TOTAL **5 MIN.**

½ cup packed light brown sugar
2 Tbsp. salted butter
2 Tbsp. heavy cream
2 Tbsp. (1 oz.) bourbon

Stir together brown sugar, butter, and heavy cream in a small saucepan. Bring to a boil over medium. Boil, stirring constantly, 1 minute. Remove from heat; stir in bourbon.

Derby Monkey Bread

Quick Kentucky
Modjeskas

SOUTHERN SIT-DOWN

The meal of the season is meant to be shared and should be so delicious that those gathered together feel compelled to linger. This menu serves up all the classics you crave with flavorful twists that make each course special for an unforgettable meal.

the menu

SERVES 10

Pecan Vodka Old-Fashioned

Parmesan-Chive Spoon Rolls

Fennel, Hazelnut, and Herb Salad

Oyster Stew with Black Pepper Cornbread Croutons

Aligot Potatoes

Raw Cranberry-Pecan Sauce

Asparagus Casserole

Dry-Brined Rosemary and Wild Mushroom Turkey

Rustic Pear-Sweet Potato Tart

The geometric forms of Canadian hemlock, boxwood, ligustrum, and Japanese yew in the Ladew topiary garden morph into a magical Christmas forest when blanketed in a carpet of snow, offering a whimsical passage to the stately home beyond.

Pecan Vodka Old-Fashioned

Consider this a lighter version of the traditional Old-Fashioned, using vodka in place of bourbon. The subtle nutty flavor is complemented nicely by a dash of bitters.

SERVES **1** ACTIVE **5 MIN.** TOTAL **5 MIN.**

2 brown sugar cubes
1 (3-in.) orange peel strip
1 tsp. orange- or cardamom-flavored bitters
1/4 cup (2 oz.) pecan-flavored vodka (such as Cathead)
1/4 cup club soda, chilled

Muddle together sugar cubes, orange peel strip, and bitters in a rocks glass. Add vodka and a few ice cubes; top with club soda, and stir gently. Serve immediately.

Parmesan-Chive Spoon Rolls

Aged Parmesan adds loads of flavor to these buttery spoon rolls dotted with green chives.

SERVES **16** ACTIVE **20 MIN.** TOTAL **40 MIN.**

Cooking spray
2 cups lukewarm water (100°F to 110°F)
1 tsp. granulated sugar
1 (1/4 oz.) envelope active dry yeast
4 cups (about 16 oz.) self-rising flour
2 oz. Parmesan cheese, finely shredded (about 3/4 cup)
3 Tbsp. finely chopped fresh chives
1/2 tsp. kosher salt
1/2 tsp. black pepper
3/4 cup (6 oz.) salted butter, melted
1 large egg, lightly beaten

1. Preheat oven to 400°F. Generously coat 2 (12-cup) muffin pans with cooking spray. Stir together water, sugar, and yeast in a large bowl; let mixture stand 5 minutes.

2. Stir together flour, cheese, chives, salt, and pepper in a bowl; add to yeast mixture. Add butter and egg; stir to combine. Spoon batter into 16 of the prepared muffin pans, filling each three-fourths full.

3. Bake in preheated oven until rolls are golden brown, 20 to 22 minutes.

Note: Unused batter may be stored in an airtight container in refrigerator up to 1 week.

Fennel, Hazelnut, and Herb Salad

Caramelized fennel, toasted nuts, and peppery arugula combine with sturdy frisée in this tasty winter salad.

SERVES **10** ACTIVE **15 MIN.** TOTAL **45 MIN.**

4 fennel bulbs, fronds reserved
1/4 cup olive oil
1/2 tsp. granulated sugar
2 tsp. kosher salt, divided
1/2 cup blanched hazelnuts (see below)
6 Tbsp. balsamic vinegar
2 Tbsp. honey
1 Tbsp. Dijon mustard
1/2 tsp. black pepper
3/4 cup hazelnut oil
6 cups baby arugula (5 oz.)
2 (5 oz. total) heads frisée, torn into bite-size pieces
1 oz. Parmesan cheese, shaved (about 1/2 cup)
1/4 cup packed fresh flat-leaf parsley leaves

1. Preheat oven to 425°F. Reserve 1/4 cup fronds from fennel bulbs; set aside, and discard remaining fronds. Trim and core fennel bulbs; set aside 1 bulb. Cut remaining 3 bulbs into 8 wedges each. Toss together fennel wedges, olive oil, sugar, and 1 teaspoon of the salt in a bowl. Arrange in a single layer on a baking sheet lined with parchment paper. Roast in preheated oven until caramelized and tender, 18 to 20 minutes, turning once halfway through roast time. Let cool completely, about 10 minutes. Thinly slice reserved fennel bulb using a mandoline; set aside.

2. Spread hazelnuts evenly in a pie plate; toast at 425°F until golden, about 6 minutes. Let cool 10 minutes; chop.

3. Stir together vinegar, honey, mustard, pepper, and remaining 1 teaspoon salt in a large bowl. Whisk in hazelnut oil. Add roasted fennel, sliced fennel, arugula, and frisée; toss to coat. Transfer to a large serving bowl. Top with fennel fronds, toasted hazelnuts, Parmesan, and parsley. Serve immediately.

Ingredients 101

Hazelnuts, also called filberts, grow on the bushy hazel shrub. This sweet, rich nut has a hard, smooth, helmet-shaped capped shell. Shelled nuts are covered in a bitter brown skin. To remove, heat the nuts at 375°F for about 10 minutes until skins start to split. Wrap the nuts in a clean (but old, as it may stain) dish towel and rub the nuts together inside the towel to remove as much of the skins as possible. Alternatively, blanch the nuts in 2 cups boiling water with 2 tablespoons baking soda for 3 to 5 minutes until skins easily come off under cold running water.

Fennel, Hazelnut, and Herb Salad

Elise

Harper

Oyster Stew with Black Pepper Cornbread Croutons

Raw Cranberry-
Pecan Sauce

Dry-Brined Rosemary
and Wild Mushroom
Turkey

Asparagus Casserole

Aligot Potatoes

Oyster Stew with Black Pepper Cornbread Croutons

This stew brims with wow factor yet is so simple to prepare. Tasty additions—crisp bacon, cornbread croutons, and tender fingerlings—add a sophisticated air to this company-worthy recipe. The oysters come packed in the collected juices from shucking. It is liquid gold, so don't discard it.

SERVES **10** ACTIVE **25 MIN.** TOTAL **55 MIN.**

12 oz. slab bacon, cut into 1-in. cubes
2 (12-oz.) containers fresh oysters, undrained
¼ cup unsalted butter
1 medium-size yellow onion, chopped (2 cups)
3 medium carrots, diced (2 cups)
2 large celery stalks, chopped (2 cups)
1 cup (8 oz.) white wine
2 qt. whipping cream
1½ lb. fingerling potatoes, cut into 1-in. cubes
1 Tbsp. kosher salt
3 medium-size plum tomatoes, chopped (2 cups)
1 tsp. black pepper
1 cup Rich Black Pepper Cornbread Croutons (recipe p. 67)
Chopped fresh chives

1. Cook bacon in a cast-iron skillet over medium, stirring occasionally, until browned and crispy, 10 to 12 minutes. Drain on paper towels.

2. Drain oysters, reserving liquid from containers; set aside.

3. Melt butter in a large Dutch oven over medium. Add onion, carrots, and celery; cook, stirring occasionally, until tender, 5 to 7 minutes. Add wine and reserved oyster liquid; let come to a simmer. Simmer, undisturbed, until liquid is reduced by half, about 5 minutes. Stir in whipping cream, potatoes, and salt; bring to a boil over high. Reduce heat to medium; simmer, undisturbed, until cream is slightly thickened and potatoes are tender, about 15 minutes. Add oysters; cook, undisturbed, until edges just begin to curl, about 3 minutes. Stir in tomatoes and pepper.

4. Remove from heat. Ladle evenly into 10 bowls. Sprinkle evenly with bacon and croutons; garnish with chives.

Aligot Potatoes

Holiday meals deserve a touch of decadence. This cheesy side dish definitely lends it. Work quickly once your potatoes are boiled. You need their heat to melt the cheese so that it fully incorporates. This is a more elegant mashed potato version of beloved Southern mac-n-cheese. Substitute russet potatoes if you wish.

SERVES **10** ACTIVE **15 MIN.** TOTAL **30 MIN.**

3 qt. water
2 lb. Yukon Gold potatoes, peeled and cut into large cubes
1 bay leaf
2 Tbsp. kosher salt, divided
12 oz. fresh mozzarella cheese, cut into ½-in. cubes
1 cup heavy cream
¼ cup unsalted butter
12 oz. Gruyère cheese, shredded (about 3 cups)
¼ tsp. freshly grated nutmeg

1. Place water, potatoes, bay leaf, and 1 tablespoon of the salt in a large saucepan. Bring to a boil over high; reduce heat to medium, and simmer until tender, 15 to 17 minutes.

2. While potatoes boil, cook mozzarella and cream in a small saucepan over medium, stirring occasionally, until bubbles form and mixture begins to steam, 6 to 7 minutes. Cover and keep warm over low.

3. Drain potatoes; discard bay leaf. Working quickly, push potatoes through a ricer back into saucepan. Add mozzarella mixture and butter; stir vigorously using a wooden spoon until fully incorporated. Stir in Gruyère, nutmeg, and remaining 1 tablespoon salt. Serve immediately.

Raw Cranberry-Pecan Sauce

Bitter citrus peel and astringent cranberries are balanced by the concentrated sweetness of raisins and a dose of Grand Marnier for a touch of sophistication. Toasty pecans and nutmeg provide tailor-made holiday flavor.

SERVES **10** ACTIVE **15 MIN.** TOTAL **45 MIN.**

2 navel oranges
1 cup raisins
1 (16-oz.) pkg. fresh cranberries
½ cup toasted pecan pieces
¼ cup granulated sugar
1 tsp. kosher salt
⅛ tsp. ground nutmeg
1 Tbsp. (½ oz.) orange liqueur (such as Grand Marnier)

1. Peel 1 orange; discard peel. (Leave remaining orange unpeeled.) Cut oranges into 8 wedges; remove and discard seeds.

2. Place orange wedges and raisins in a food processor; pulse until roughly chopped, about 6 times. Add cranberries, pecans, sugar, salt, and nutmeg; pulse until finely chopped but not pureed, about 6 times.

3. Transfer mixture to a serving bowl; stir in liqueur. Cover and refrigerate at least 30 minutes or up to 24 hours.

Asparagus Casserole

Surprise and delight your guests with this unexpected swap in the traditional green bean casserole. Asparagus spears play well with the creamy, cheesy mushroom sauce. Use medium-thick spears here. Thin ones will fall apart.

SERVES **10** ACTIVE **20 MIN.** TOTAL **1 HOUR**

3 lb. fresh asparagus, trimmed
$1/2$ cup (4 oz.) salted butter, divided
1 (8-oz.) pkg. sliced fresh cremini mushrooms, roughly chopped
1 large shallot, chopped (3 Tbsp.)
6 Tbsp. all-purpose flour
4 cups whole milk
4 oz. Parmesan cheese, shredded (about 1$1/2$ cups)
2 tsp. kosher salt
$1/2$ tsp. black pepper
$1/2$ cup crispy fried shallots (about 2 oz.)
$1/2$ cup toasted sliced almonds

1. Preheat oven to 350°F. Bring a large pot of salted water to a boil over high. Add asparagus; cook 2 minutes. Drain; rinse under cold water, and drain again. Drain on paper towels.

2. Heat 2 tablespoons of the butter in a Dutch oven over medium-high. Add mushrooms and shallot; cook, stirring often, until mixture is deeply browned and caramelized, about 10 minutes. Transfer mixture to a plate. Add remaining 6 tablespoons butter to Dutch oven; melt over medium-high. Whisk in flour; cook, whisking constantly, 1 minute. Gradually add milk, whisking until smooth. Cook, whisking constantly, until thickened and bubbly, about 4 minutes. Remove from heat; whisk in cheese, salt, and pepper until melted and smooth. Stir in asparagus and mushroom mixture; spoon mixture into a 13- x 9-inch baking dish.

3. Bake in preheated oven until bubbly around edges, about 25 minutes. Remove from oven; sprinkle with fried shallots and almonds. Return to oven; continue baking until topping is golden brown, about 5 minutes.

Make Ahead: Prepare recipe as directed through Step 2. Cover mixture, and refrigerate up to 3 days. Bake at 350°F for about 35 minutes. Add fried shallots and almonds; continue baking until topping is golden brown, about 10 minutes.

Dry-Brined Rosemary and Wild Mushroom Turkey

Dry brining allows the seasonings to really meld with the natural juices in the meat for more concentrated flavor and crispy skin. If you opt to use porcini powder in this recipe, you may need to adjust the salt in the recipe; the powder may contain added salt.

SERVES **8 TO 10** ACTIVE **25 MIN.**
TOTAL **13 HOURS, 25 MIN., INCLUDING 10 HOURS CHILLING**

1 oz. dried porcini mushrooms
$1/2$ cup loosely packed fresh rosemary leaves (from 3 sprigs)
3 Tbsp. kosher salt
3 Tbsp. dark brown sugar
1$1/2$ tsp. black pepper
1 tsp. garlic powder
1 (12- to 14-lb.) whole fresh or thawed frozen turkey
$1/2$ cup (4 oz.) unsalted butter, softened
Cooking spray

1. Process dried mushrooms, rosemary leaves, salt, sugar, pepper, and garlic powder in a food processor until mixture is ground and combined, about 45 seconds.

2. Remove giblets and neck from turkey; discard or reserve for another use. Pat turkey dry. Measure 1 tablespoon brine mixture (powdered mushroom mixture) into a small bowl, and set aside. Rub 1 tablespoon brine mixture into turkey cavity. Sprinkle outside of turkey with remaining brine mixture; rub into skin. Chill turkey, uncovered, at least 10 hours or up to 24 hours.

3. Preheat oven to 350°F. Stir together butter and reserved 1 tablespoon brine mixture in a small bowl. Loosen skin from turkey breast (without totally detaching skin); spread butter mixture under skin. Replace skin, securing with wooden picks.

4. Tie ends of legs together with kitchen twine; tuck wing tips under. Place turkey, breast side up, on a lightly greased (with cooking spray) rack set inside a large roasting pan.

5. Bake in preheated oven until a thermometer inserted in thickest portion of turkey thigh registers 165°F, about 2 hours, 30 minutes. Remove from oven; let stand 30 minutes. Carve and serve.

Rustic Pear-Sweet Potato Tart

This delectable pairing of sweet potatoes and Bartlett pears is not overly sweet, which allows the flavors to shine. The candied pecans add a wonderful crunch. If you have any, leftovers are delicious on salads and ice cream—or simply for snacking.

SERVES **10** ACTIVE **30 MIN.** TOTAL **4 HOURS**

TART
2 large (about 1½ lb. total) sweet potatoes
3 Tbsp. unsalted butter
¼ cup packed light brown sugar
¼ cup, plus 1 tsp. granulated sugar, divided
2 tsp. fresh lemon juice (from 1 lemon)
1 tsp. ground cinnamon
¼ tsp. ground nutmeg
4 medium (about 1½ lb. total) firm Bartlett pears, peeled and cut into ¼-in.-thick slices
1 Tbsp. cornstarch
½ (14.1-oz.) pkg. refrigerated piecrusts
1 tsp. ice water

CANDIED PECANS
¼ cup granulated sugar
¼ tsp. ground cinnamon
Pinch of table salt
1 cup roughly chopped pecans
Cooking spray

1. Prepare the Tart: Preheat oven to 400°F. Pierce sweet potatoes several times all over using a fork. Place on a baking sheet lined with aluminum foil. Bake in preheated oven 30 minutes. Remove from oven (and turn off oven); let cool 20 minutes. Peel and cut into ¼-inch-thick slices.

2. Melt butter in a large skillet over medium-high. Add brown sugar and ¼ cup of the granulated sugar; cook, stirring constantly, until sugars dissolve, about 2 minutes. Stir in sweet potatoes, lemon juice, cinnamon, and nutmeg. Cover and reduce heat to medium-low; cook 10 minutes. Uncover and stir in pears; cook, stirring occasionally, until sweet potatoes and pears are tender, about 10 minutes. Remove from heat. Measure 3 tablespoons cooking liquid from skillet into a small bowl; whisk in cornstarch. Stir cornstarch mixture back into sweet potato mixture in skillet. Let cool to room temperature, about 30 minutes.

3. Preheat oven to 400°F with rack in lower-third position. Place piecrust on a piece of parchment paper, and roll into a 14-inch circle. Transfer dough and parchment paper onto a baking sheet. Arrange cooled sweet potato mixture in center of dough, leaving a 2-inch border. Fold dough edges up and in toward center, pressing gently to seal (dough will only partially cover the sweet potato mixture). Brush dough with ice water, and sprinkle evenly with remaining 1 teaspoon granulated sugar. Bake in preheated oven until crust is golden brown and filling is bubbly, about 45 minutes. Transfer to a wire rack; let cool at least 1 hour or until completely cool (about 2 hours).

4. While Tart cools, prepare the Candied Pecans: Stir together sugar, cinnamon, and pinch of salt in a heavy saucepan over medium. Add pecans; cook, stirring constantly, until sugar melts and coats pecans, 7 to 8 minutes. (Sugar will appear grainy before it melts and coats pecans.) Spread evenly on a piece of wax paper coated with cooking spray; let cool 20 minutes.

5. To serve, sprinkle Tart with ½ cup Candied Pecans (remaining pecans may be stored in an airtight container up to 1 week).

GULF COAST TOAST

Inspired by the exotic ingredients and spices that come into Southern ports of call within the Gulf of Mexico, this cocktail party menu takes you on a delicious journey into the New Year with a melting pot of Far East flavors married with some of our favorite Southern standards.

the menu

SERVES 12

Spirited Port of Call Sparklers

Marinated Olives and Mushrooms

Black-Eyed Pea Pâté with Crudités

Pork Wontons with Sesame-Soy Dipping Sauce

Old Bay Cheese Straws

Shrimp Toast

Korean Meatballs

Green Tea Shortbread

Like the pop of a Champagne cork or the burst of a colorful confetti shower, fireworks at the beach are a showstopping finale to any New Year's Eve bash. After all, new beginnings should always be a blast.

Spirited Port of Call Sparklers

This bubbly spin on the classic Port of Call cocktail swaps sweet sparkling red wine for the usual port in a tipple tailor-made for toasting.

SERVES **1**   ACTIVE **5 MIN.**   TOTAL **5 MIN.**

1 oz. gin
½ oz. fresh lemon juice
½ oz. cinnamon syrup
1 tsp. cranberry preserves
3 oz. chilled sweet sparkling Italian red wine (such as Lambrusco amabile)
Frozen blackberries or raspberries

Combine gin, lemon juice, cinnamon syrup, and cranberry preserves in a cocktail shaker. Shake vigorously. Strain into a Champagne flute. Top with the sparkling red wine. Drop a few frozen berries into the glass to keep the drink chilled.

Marinated Olives and Mushrooms

This easy, make-ahead medley was well received in our Test Kitchen. The olives and mushrooms really soak up the flavorful marinade. Look for pitted Castelvetrano olives in jars or in the antipasti section of your local grocery store. If you can't find the pitted variety, then leave the pits in and provide a small bowl for your guests to discard them.

SERVES **12**   ACTIVE **15 MIN.**   TOTAL **8 HOURS, 45 MIN.**

3 cups pitted Castelvetrano or Cerignola olives
    (about 15 oz.)
2 cups small button mushrooms, trimmed and washed
    (about 6 oz.)
6 Tbsp. extra-virgin olive oil
2 Tbsp. toasted sesame oil
1 Tbsp. orange zest plus 2 Tbsp. fresh juice (from 1 orange)
1 Tbsp. lemon zest plus 1 Tbsp. fresh juice (from 1 lemon)
1 Tbsp. minced garlic (about 3 garlic cloves)
1 tsp. coarsely crushed coriander seeds
½ tsp. crushed red pepper

Stir together all ingredients in a large bowl. Cover and chill 8 hours. Let stand 30 minutes at room temperature before serving. Serve mixture with a slotted spoon. Store olives in an airtight container in the refrigerator up to 1 week.

Marinated Olives and Mushrooms

Old Bay Cheese
Straws

Black-Eyed Pea Pâté with Crudités

Pork Wontons with Sesame-Soy Dipping Sauce

Black-Eyed Pea Pâté with Crudités

It's rare to find a Southerner who doesn't make sure to eat at least a spoonful of black-eyed peas for good luck in the New Year. This creamy pea pâté makes it deliciously easy to get your dose. This is best made ahead so that it's nice and cold when ready to serve and so the flavors have time to come together.

MAKES **2 CUPS** ACTIVE **25 MIN.**
TOTAL **8 HOURS, 35 MIN.**

1/2 cup olive oil, divided
3/4 cup chopped Chinese lap cheong dried sausage
   (about 3 oz.)
1 (3.5-oz.) pkg. fresh shiitake mushrooms, sliced
   (or 4 oz. sliced fresh button mushrooms)
3 garlic cloves, chopped
1 serrano chile, seeded and finely chopped
3 Tbsp. mirin
1/4 cup chicken stock
1 (15-oz.) can black-eyed peas, drained and rinsed
1/2 cup roasted, salted peanuts
1/2 cup chopped fresh cilantro
1/4 tsp. kosher salt
Pickled Shallots and Cucumbers (recipe follows)
Crudités (such as sugar snap peas, snow peas, carrot
   sticks, celery sticks), for serving
Baguette slices, for serving

1. Heat 2 tablespoons of the oil in a large skillet over medium-high. Add sausage, mushrooms, garlic, and serrano, and cook, stirring often, until lightly browned, 4 to 5 minutes. Stir in mirin, and cook, stirring occasionally, 1 minute. Add chicken stock, and stir to combine. Stir in peas.

2. Transfer mixture to a food processor; add peanuts and remaining 6 tablespoons olive oil, and process just until smooth, about 1 minute. Add cilantro and salt, and pulse to combine, about 5 times. Cover and chill at least 8 hours or up to 24 hours.

3. Transfer to a shallow bowl. Top with desired amount of drained Pickled Shallots and Cucumbers. Serve with choice of crudités and baguette slices.

Ingredients 101

Find Chinese lap cheong dried sausage packaged in links at your Asian market. The name translates to "wax sausage," which is a nod to its waxy appearance. Though it may be cooked and eaten on its own, it is traditionally used as a seasoning or flavoring in dishes.

Pickled Shallots and Cucumbers

MAKES **2 CUPS** ACTIVE **10 MIN.**
TOTAL **2 HOURS, 10 MIN.**

2 Persian cucumbers (or baby seedless cucumbers),
   seeded and sliced
1 garlic clove, minced
1 cup thinly sliced shallots (about 3 medium shallots [3 oz.
   total])
1 cup seasoned rice wine vinegar
1/4 cup water
1 Tbsp. granulated sugar
1 1/2 tsp. table salt
Toasted sesame oil
Toasted sesame seeds

Stir together cucumbers, garlic, shallots, vinegar, water, sugar, and salt in a large bowl. Cover and chill at least 2 hours or up to 2 days. Drizzle with toasted sesame oil, and sprinkle with toasted sesame seeds just before serving.

Pork Wontons with Sesame-Soy Dipping Sauce

These potstickers are paired with a perfectly balanced sauce that blends the sweetness of brown sugar with the acidity of vinegar and lime. We tested this recipe with Annie Chun's potstickers, but feel free to use whatever brand you prefer. The sauce will keep in the fridge for up to 1 week. It's delicious with sushi or rice noodles too.

SERVES **12** ACTIVE **10 MIN.** TOTAL **10 MIN.**

3 Tbsp. rice wine vinegar
2 Tbsp. lower-sodium soy sauce or tamari
1 Tbsp. thinly sliced scallion (from 1 scallion)
1 Tbsp. fresh lime juice (from 1 lime)
1 1/2 tsp. minced garlic
1 tsp. minced fresh ginger
1 tsp. light brown sugar
1 tsp. Asian chile-garlic sauce
1/2 tsp. dark sesame oil
2 (19-oz.) pkg. frozen pork- or chicken-and-vegetable
   potstickers (about 32 total), prepared according to pkg.
   directions

Whisk together vinegar, soy sauce, scallion, lime juice, garlic, ginger, brown sugar, chile-garlic sauce, and sesame oil in a small bowl. Serve with hot potstickers.

Old Bay Cheese Straws

A touch of crab boil seasoning adds a dose of beachy flavor to the classic cheese straw. These are delicious as an appetizer but also wonderful in place of bread with a salad course or with a creamy shrimp rémoulade.

SERVES **12**   ACTIVE **30 MIN.**   TOTAL **45 MIN.**

½ (17.3-oz.) pkg. frozen puff pastry sheets, thawed
All-purpose flour, for work surface and sprinkling dough
2 Tbsp. extra-virgin olive oil
4 tsp. Old Bay seasoning
1 oz. Parmesan cheese, finely grated (about ¼ cup)
1 large egg
2 Tbsp. water

1. Preheat oven to 375°F. Unfold pastry sheet, and place on a lightly floured work surface. Lightly flour a rolling pin, and roll pastry sheet into a 12- x 8-inch (about ⅛-inch-thick) rectangle with horizontal long edges. Evenly trim edges.

2. Brush top of pastry all over with 1 tablespoon of the olive oil. Sprinkle right half of pastry with 2 teaspoons of the Old Bay seasoning and 2 tablespoons of the cheese. Fold left half of pastry (unsprinkled side) over seasoned half (like closing a book). Lightly sprinkle top of pastry with flour, and roll back out into a 12- x 8-inch rectangle. Brush top of pastry all over with remaining 1 tablespoon olive oil. Sprinkle right half with remaining Old Bay seasoning and cheese, and fold left half over. Roll into an 8- x 6-inch rectangle.

3. Using a sharp knife, cut pastry lengthwise into ⅓-inch-wide strips; cut strips in half. Loosely twist each strip a couple of times, forming a spiral, and place on ungreased baking sheets. Gently press ends on baking sheet to keep straw from untwisting. Stir together egg and water in a small bowl; lightly brush tops of strips with egg wash.

4. Bake in preheated oven until light golden brown, 12 to 15 minutes. Let cool 1 minute on baking sheets. Using a spatula, gently loosen straws from baking sheet, and serve warm or at room temperature.

Tip

Old Bay seasoning is a commercially prepared spice blend consisting of celery salt, dry mustard, and paprika that originated in the Chesapeake Bay area and is often used in the preparation of shellfish. You can substitute dry seasoning blends labeled Crab Boil, Shrimp Boil, or Seafood Boil for the Old Bay called for here.

Shrimp Toast

Pickled, fried, or barbecued, we love our shrimp in the South. This shrimp paste slathered on crispy toasts with pickled ginger is guaranteed to knock your guests' socks off! Consider garnishing a platter of these with something green—chopped fresh scallions, basil, or cilantro. We liked sliced white bread for this. The most involved part of this recipe is smearing the shrimp mixture onto the bread slices, but it's so simple that you can ask your kids to help.

SERVES **12**   ACTIVE **30 MIN.**   TOTAL **30 MIN.**

2 lb. peeled and deveined raw medium shrimp, patted dry with paper towels
½ cup chopped scallions (about 3 to 4 scallions), plus more for garnish
2 tsp. shichimi (nanami) togarashi
1 tsp. lime zest plus 1½ Tbsp. fresh juice (from 1 lime)
2 tsp. toasted sesame seeds, plus more for garnish
Vegetable oil
12 white sandwich bread slices (such as Pepperidge Farm), crusts removed
48 pickled ginger slices

1. Combine shrimp, scallions, togarashi, lime zest, lime juice, and sesame seeds in a food processor; pulse until thoroughly chopped, about 10 times. Set shrimp mixture aside. Pour oil to a depth of 2 inches in a Dutch oven; heat over medium-high to 350°F.

2. While oil heats, spread about 3 tablespoons shrimp mixture (about a ½-inch-thick layer) on each bread slice. Cut each slice into quarters.

3. Fry squares in hot oil, shrimp sides down, in batches of 6, until shrimp mixture inflates, about 1 minute. Flip squares over, and fry until bread is lightly browned and toasted, about 30 seconds.

4. Remove toasts from oil, and pat dry with paper towels. Top pieces evenly with pickled ginger slices; sprinkle with scallions and sesame seeds. Serve immediately.

Korean Meatballs

A collision of spicy and sweet from the gochujang, honey, and ketchup makes these meatballs a deliciously easy and creative appetizer. Because the dish is so saucy, serve it in a bowl. Browning the meatballs gives them texture. Be sure to deglaze the pan and combine the flavorful bits into the sauce to give it added complexity. These meatballs are a terrific party appetizer but are also sensational served over rice or in a Korean-inspired meatball sub.

SERVES **12**   ACTIVE **30 MIN.**   TOTAL **1 HOUR**

MEATBALLS
1¼ lb. ground beef
2 Tbsp. minced fresh scallions (from 2 scallions)
1 Tbsp. minced garlic (from 3 garlic cloves)
1 Tbsp. minced fresh ginger
1 Tbsp. soy sauce or tamari
1 Tbsp. fish sauce
1 Tbsp. mirin
1 Tbsp. seasoned rice vinegar

SAUCE
¾ cup ketchup
⅓ cup gochujang
¼ cup mirin
2 Tbsp. honey
1 Tbsp. grated fresh ginger

ADDITIONAL INGREDIENTS
2 Tbsp. sesame oil
2 Tbsp. water
Sesame seeds (optional)

1. Prepare the Meatballs: Using your hands, gently mix together beef, scallions, garlic, ginger, soy sauce, fish sauce, mirin, and vinegar in a large bowl until incorporated. Form mixture into 36 balls (about 1 tablespoon each). Refrigerate 20 minutes.

2. Prepare the Sauce: While Meatballs chill, stir together ketchup, gochujang, mirin, honey, and ginger in a medium bowl. Set aside.

3. Cook the Meatballs: Heat 2 teaspoons of the sesame oil in a large, high-sided skillet over medium-high. Add about 12 Meatballs; cook until browned on 2 sides, about 2 minutes per side. Remove Meatballs from skillet. Repeat with remaining 24 Meatballs and 4 teaspoons oil.

4. Add Sauce and water to skillet, and bring to a simmer over medium-high. Return Meatballs to skillet; reduce heat to medium-low, and cover. Simmer until Meatballs are cooked through, about 6 minutes. Sprinkle with sesame seeds, if desired.

Green Tea Shortbread

These cookies garnered oohs and aahs in our Test Kitchen. They are very "short," or crumbly, with a pleasing nutty flavor that is not overly sweet. Matcha powder is readily available these days. Look in the health food aisle of your grocery store or in the section with tea and coffee. Enjoy these healthy cookies on their own, with a cup of hot tea, or with an ice cold glass of milk.

MAKES **4 DOZEN**   ACTIVE **30 MIN.**
TOTAL **2 HOURS, 15 MIN.**

2½ cups (about 10⅝ oz.) all-purpose flour
2 Tbsp. cornstarch
2 Tbsp. matcha green tea powder
1 cup (8 oz.) unsalted butter, slightly softened
¾ cup (about 3 oz.) powdered sugar
½ tsp. table salt
1 cup granulated sugar, for coating

1. Whisk together flour, cornstarch, and matcha powder in a medium bowl. Beat butter, powdered sugar, and salt in a heavy-duty stand mixer fitted with paddle attachment on medium speed 2 minutes. Add flour mixture all at once, and beat on low speed just until incorporated, 1 to 2 minutes. Pat dough into an 8-inch-wide disk, wrap in plastic wrap, and refrigerate until just firm, about 15 minutes.

2. Place dough disk between 2 sheets of parchment paper on a work surface, and roll to a ¼-inch-thick round. Slide dough round and parchment paper pieces onto a baking sheet, and refrigerate until firm, about 15 minutes.

3. Meanwhile, preheat oven to 325°F. Slide dough round and parchment paper pieces back to work surface. Peel top sheet of parchment paper off dough, and discard. Prick top of disk all over with a fork. Using a 2-inch fluted round cutter, cut out cookies, as close together as possible, and arrange 1 inch apart on parchment paper-lined baking sheets. Refrigerate cookies. Reroll dough scraps between sheets of parchment paper to ¼-inch-thickness, and refrigerate until firm, about 10 minutes. Cut out cookies, and arrange on baking sheets.

4. Bake in preheated oven on upper and middle racks 20 minutes. Reduce oven temperature to 250°F. Shift baking sheets from top to bottom and front to back, and bake until golden brown, about 10 minutes. Let cookies cool on baking sheets 2 minutes; then transfer to a wire rack.

5. Place granulated sugar in a shallow bowl. Carefully place warm cookies in sugar, and turn to coat. Transfer to rack, and let cool completely, about 30 minutes.

Shrimp
Toast

Korean Meatballs

Green Tea
Shortbread

Jamaican Jerk Roasted Cornish Hens

RUBBED & ROASTED

Holiday dinners are a marker of time in the life of a family. We look back and remember the conversations, the decorations, and all the wonderful food on the table. The centerpiece of any legendary holiday meal is the roast. Whether you prize succulent turf or tender surf, these company-worthy options are bathed in flavorful herb and spice medleys guaranteed to make them memorable.

featuring

Jamaican Jerk Roasted Cornish Hens

Peppercorn-and-Coriander Roasted Pork Tenderloins

Citrus-Herb-Rubbed Whole Fish

Coffee-Rubbed Rib-Eye Roast

Berbere-Spiced Leg of Lamb

Jamaican Jerk Roasted Cornish Hens

These mini roasted gems come together in a flash after the spice mix rub is made, so you can enjoy your guests while the hens roast and make the house smell heavenly.

SERVES **4**   ACTIVE **15 MIN.**   TOTAL **50 MIN.**

SPICE MIXTURE
¼ cup olive oil
1 Tbsp. dried parsley
1 Tbsp. dried onion flakes
1 Tbsp. light brown sugar
2 tsp. cayenne pepper
2 tsp. garlic powder
2 tsp. ground thyme
1½ tsp. kosher salt
1 tsp. crushed red pepper
1 tsp. ground allspice
½ tsp. freshly grated nutmeg
½ tsp. black pepper
½ tsp. ground cinnamon
ADDITIONAL INGREDIENTS
2 (1½-lb.) Cornish hens
Cooking spray

1. Preheat oven to 400°F. Prepare the Spice Mixture: Stir together all ingredients in a bowl. Set aside.

2. Remove giblets and necks from hens, and reserve for another use. Rinse hens under cold water; pat dry. Remove and discard skin; trim excess fat. Split hens in half lengthwise. Rub evenly all over with Spice Mixture.

3. Place hen halves, breast sides up, in a shallow roasting pan coated with cooking spray. Insert a thermometer into meaty part of a thigh, avoiding the bone. Roast in preheated oven until thermometer registers 165°F, about 35 minutes. Transfer hens to a platter; cover with aluminum foil. Let rest 5 minutes. Serve.

Peppercorn-and-Coriander Roasted Pork Tenderloins

This flavorful rub makes everyday pork tenderloins stand outs. Be sure to preheat your skillet to ensure optimal browning and all the crusty flavor that comes with it.

SERVES **8**   ACTIVE **20 MIN.**   TOTAL **1 HOUR, 10 MIN.**

2 Tbsp. coriander seeds
1 Tbsp. black peppercorns
2 Tbsp. honey mustard
2 tsp. kosher salt
2 (1-lb.) pork tenderloins, trimmed
1 Tbsp. olive oil

1. Cook coriander seeds and peppercorns in a small skillet over medium, stirring occasionally, until fragrant, about 4 minutes. Remove from heat; let cool 10 minutes. Coarsely crush using a mortar and pestle (or transfer to a ziplock plastic bag, and crush using the bottom of a heavy skillet).

2. Preheat oven to 350°F. Stir together mustard, salt, and crushed spices in a small bowl. Rub mixture evenly over pork tenderloins. Let stand 20 minutes.

3. Heat oil in a large ovenproof skillet over medium-high. Add pork; cook 5 minutes, turning to brown on all sides.

4. Transfer skillet to preheated oven; roast until a thermometer inserted in thickest portion of meat registers 145°F (slightly pink), 12 to 15 minutes, turning after 7 minutes. Remove from oven; let rest 10 minutes. Cut pork crosswise into ½-inch-thick slices.

Peppercorn-and-Coriander
Roasted Pork Tenderloins

Citrus-Herb-Rubbed Whole Fish

Citrus-Herb-Rubbed Whole Fish

Order your fish "dressed" (cleaned, scaled, and fins trimmed). Don't cut too deep when scoring the fish. You want to cut just through the skin to keep the fish from curling up as it cooks. Citrus and fennel are classics with fish and add aromatic flavor to this sweet, flaky fish.

SERVES **4**   ACTIVE **15 MIN.**   TOTAL **45 MIN.**

2 Tbsp. orange zest (from 1 large orange)
2 Tbsp. lemon zest, plus 3 Tbsp. fresh juice (from 2 lemons), divided
1 tsp. black pepper
2 Tbsp., plus 1/4 tsp. kosher salt, divided
1 large fennel bulb, fronds reserved
2 Tbsp. extra-virgin olive oil, divided
6 medium garlic cloves, minced (1 Tbsp.)
Cooking spray
2 (1³/₄-lb.) whole striped bass, cleaned and scaled (heads and tails intact)
1 orange, cut into 8 slices

1. Process orange zest, lemon zest, pepper, and 2 tablespoons of the salt in a mini food processor until finely ground, about 1 minute. Set aside.

2. Preheat oven to 400°F. Finely chop fennel fronds to measure 1 tablespoon; set aside. Thinly slice fennel bulb. Heat a large nonstick skillet over medium-high. Add 1 tablespoon of the oil; swirl to coat. Add sliced fennel and garlic; cook, stirring often, until lightly browned, about 6 minutes. Stir in remaining 1/4 teaspoon salt. Remove from heat; let cool 5 minutes.

3. Line a jelly-roll pan with parchment paper; coat with cooking spray. Score skin of each fish with 3 diagonal cuts. Whisk together lemon juice and remaining 1 tablespoon oil in a bowl. Rub inside flesh of fish evenly with half of the lemon-oil mixture; drizzle outside of fish evenly with remaining lemon-oil mixture. Sprinkle inside flesh of each fish with 2 teaspoons of the reserved zest mixture. Place fish on prepared jellyroll pan. Place half of fennel-garlic mixture and 4 orange slices inside each fish. Sprinkle outside of each fish with 1½ teaspoons of the zest mixture. (Reserve remaining zest mixture for another use.)

4. Roast in preheated oven until fish flakes easily when tested with a fork, about 20 minutes. Remove from oven; let rest 5 minutes. Sprinkle with reserved fennel fronds.

Coffee-Rubbed Rib-Eye Roast

This is elegant and so delicious! The spice mixture is a great combo of peppery and sweet with wonderful notes of smoke and coffee. Make sure your butcher doesn't trim away too much fat from the roast. It insulates the meat during smoking and keeps it tender. Coating the roast with the spices right when you remove it from the refrigerator to come to room temperature really helps the flavors fuse with the meat before roasting.

SERVES **12**   ACTIVE **15 MIN.**   TOTAL **4 HOURS, 15 MIN.**

2 Tbsp. kosher salt
1 Tbsp. ground coffee beans
1 Tbsp. dark brown sugar
2 tsp. smoked paprika
2 tsp. ancho chile powder
1 tsp. garlic powder
1 tsp. onion powder
1 tsp. ground cumin
1 tsp. black pepper
1 (4-lb.) boneless rib-eye roast

1. Preheat oven to 225°F. Stir together salt, coffee, sugar, paprika, chile powder, garlic powder, onion powder, cumin, and pepper in a bowl. Pat beef dry; rub all over with coffee mixture. Let stand 30 minutes. Wrap roast loosely in aluminum foil; place on a rimmed baking sheet.

2. Bake in preheated oven until a thermometer inserted in thickest portion of meat registers 120°F (for rare) or 125°F (for medium-rare), 3 to 3½ hours.

3. Remove from oven; let rest 30 minutes. Unwrap roast, reserving juices. Cut into ½-inch-thick slices; serve with juices.

Berbere-Spiced Leg of Lamb

The unique flavor of lamb pairs well with strong spices, and this classic North African blend is an ideal match. The spices roast with the meat at high temperature in the oven, bringing out their distinctive flavor profiles. Collect the berbere-spiced meat juices on the cutting board to spoon back over the sliced meat as an aromatic sauce.

SERVES **8**   ACTIVE **20 MIN.**   TOTAL **3 HOURS**

SPICE MIXTURE
3 Tbsp. paprika
1 Tbsp. crushed red pepper
1 Tbsp. ground ginger
1 Tbsp. kosher salt
2 tsp. cumin seeds
1 tsp. ground turmeric
1 tsp. coriander seeds
1 tsp. ground cardamom
1 tsp. ground cinnamon

1 tsp. ground allspice
1 tsp. black pepper

ADDITIONAL INGREDIENTS
1 (5-lb.) boneless leg of lamb, rolled
   and tied
2 lb. new potatoes, halved
¼ cup olive oil
1½ tsp. kosher salt
½ tsp. black pepper

1. Prepare the Spice Mixture: Stir together all ingredients in a small bowl.

2. Rub lamb all over with Spice Mixture; let stand 1 hour.

3. Preheat oven to 450°F. Place lamb in a roasting pan. Roast in preheated oven 30 minutes. Toss together potatoes, oil, salt, and pepper in a bowl. Scatter around lamb in pan. Continue roasting at 450°F until a thermometer inserted into thickest portion of meat registers 125°F (for rare), 30 to 40 minutes.

4. Transfer lamb to a cutting board; cover loosely with aluminum foil, and let rest 15 minutes. Carve lamb; serve with potatoes.

Ingredients 101

Knowing where each cut of lamb comes from will help you understand how tender it will be and the best method of cooking it. While all cuts of lamb are relatively tender because they come from a young animal, the tenderest cuts come from the lightly used muscles along the upper back (rib and loin sections); the less tender cuts come from the more heavily used muscles (shoulder, leg, foreshank, and breast). Except for the shank cuts, you may use dry-heat cooking methods for the most part. Here are some guidelines by cut:

Shoulder: a large cut that yields firm but flavorful meat, including blade and arm chops that can be grilled or broiled, and shoulder roasts for roasting or braising

Rib: This cut also yields tender meat, including rib chops for sautéing, broiling, or grilling, as well as the crown roast.

Loin: the most tender and prized meat, and includes the loin roast and loin chops; best broiled, grilled, or sautéed

Leg: The firm but flavorful meat from this cut is roasted whole or cut into cubes for kabobs or stew. A small leg of lamb can be boned, butterflied, marinated, or grilled.

Foreshank and Breast: This meat is fatty but flavorful and includes the spareribs, which should be braised, broiled, or roasted, and riblets, which should be braised, broiled, or cooked in liquid.

Cauliflower-Potato Casserole

SIMPLE SIDES

*While the Christmas roast may be considered the star of a holiday table,
the side dishes are more than just backup singers. They are key to making
a meal a showstopper, plus they make up the bulk of every dinner plate.*

featuring

Herb-Roasted Parsnips

Cauliflower-Potato Casserole

Sugar Snap Peas with Satsuma Crumbs

Green Beans with Toasted Garlic

Caramelized Pearl Onions

Gingered Broccoli Rabe

Roasted Acorn Squash with Browned Butter

Herb-Roasted Parsnips

The nuttiness of browned butter complements the concentrated sweetness of these roasted roots that are a nice change from the usual carrots. Watch your butter closely so that it doesn't burn and transfer it immediately to a large bowl to stop the cooking when it is browned.

SERVES **6** ACTIVE **15 MIN.** TOTAL **40 MIN.**

2 lb. parsnips, cut diagonally into 2-in. pieces
2 Tbsp. olive oil
1 Tbsp. chopped fresh sage
1/2 tsp. kosher salt
1/2 tsp. black pepper
1/4 cup salted butter

1. Preheat oven to 400°F. Toss together parsnips, oil, sage, salt, and pepper in a large bowl until coated. Spread mixture evenly on a rimmed baking sheet lined with aluminum foil.

2. Bake in preheated oven until lightly browned and tender, about 25 minutes, stirring once after 15 minutes.

3. Melt butter in a small skillet over medium. Continue cooking, stirring occasionally, until brown and fragrant, 3 to 5 minutes.

4. Toss together roasted parsnip mixture and browned butter in a large bowl. Serve immediately.

Cauliflower-Potato Casserole

An extra serving of vegetables is folded into these creamy mashed potatoes. Serve with beef tenderloin or a pork roast for an impressive meal.

SERVES **10** ACTIVE **20 MIN.** TOTAL **1 HOUR, 5 MIN.**

Cooking spray
2 1/2 lb. russet potatoes, peeled and cubed
1 1/2 lb. cauliflower florets
3 1/2 tsp. kosher salt, divided
1/2 cup (4 oz.) salted butter, cut into 1/2-in. slices
4 large eggs
1 cup heavy cream
1/2 tsp. black pepper
3 oz. Parmesan cheese, finely shredded (about 1 1/3 cups)

1. Preheat oven to 350°F. Lightly coat a 13- x 9-inch baking dish with cooking spray; set aside. Place potatoes and cauliflower in a large pot; add cold water to cover. Bring to a boil over medium-high; add 2 teaspoons of the salt. Boil until tender when pierced with a knife, about 20 minutes. Drain well; return to pot.

2. Add butter to potato mixture; mash until smooth and free of lumps. Whisk together eggs, cream, pepper, and remaining 1 1/2 teaspoons salt in a bowl; add to potato mixture, and stir well to combine.

3. Spoon mixture into prepared baking dish. Bake in preheated oven 20 minutes. Remove from oven; sprinkle with cheese. Return to oven, and continue baking at 350°F until casserole is set and light golden, 15 to 20 minutes.

Sugar Snap Peas with Satsuma Crumbs

The light dressing lets the sweet snap peas' flavor shine through, while the crispy panko crumbs add welcome crunch. This recipe is easily scaled down if you are feeding a smaller crowd.

SERVES **10** ACTIVE **15 MIN.** TOTAL **35 MIN.**

1/3 cup panko (Japanese-style breadcrumbs)
2 1/2 Tbsp. extra-virgin olive oil, divided
1 tsp. clementine zest, plus 1 tsp. fresh juice (from 1 clementine), divided
1/2 tsp., plus 1/8 tsp. kosher salt, divided
1/4 tsp., plus 1/8 tsp. black pepper, divided
2 1/2 lb. fresh sugar snap peas

1. Cook panko and 1/2 tablespoon of the oil in a small skillet over medium, stirring constantly, 3 minutes. Stir in zest and 1/8 teaspoon each of the salt and pepper. Cook, stirring constantly, until golden, 2 to 3 minutes. Spoon mixture into a small bowl; set aside.

2. Fill a large pot with water to 1-inch depth; fit a steamer basket inside pot. Bring to a boil over medium-high. Reduce heat to medium. Add peas to steamer basket; cover and cook until tender-crisp, 10 to 12 minutes, stirring once halfway through cook time. Remove from heat.

3. Whisk together clementine juice and the remaining 2 tablespoons oil, 1/2 teaspoon salt, and 1/4 teaspoon pepper in a large bowl. Add peas; toss to coat. Transfer to a shallow bowl or serving platter. Sprinkle with panko mixture; serve immediately.

Herb-Roasted Parsnips

Sugar Snap Peas with
Satsuma Crumbs

Green Beans with Toasted Garlic

Packaged, pre-washed French green beans are a welcome convenience that cooks in minutes. The fragrant garlic oil and toasted garlic bits add lots of flavor and nutty texture to this vegetable mainstay of the holiday table.

SERVES **8**   ACTIVE **10 MIN.**   TOTAL **30 MIN.**

2 lb. fresh haricots verts (French green beans)
2 cups water
2 tsp. kosher salt
¹/₃ cup vegetable oil
2 Tbsp. finely chopped garlic (from 3 large garlic cloves)

1. Place green beans, water, and salt in a Dutch oven; bring to a boil over medium-high. Reduce heat to medium; cover and cook until desired degree of doneness, 3 to 5 minutes. Drain well.

2. Heat oil in a small saucepan over medium-low. Add garlic; cook, stirring often, until golden brown and crunchy, 5 to 7 minutes. (Reduce heat as needed if garlic is darkening too quickly. Do not overcook or garlic will become acrid.) Pour garlic-oil mixture through a fine-mesh strainer into a small heatproof bowl; reserve oil, and drain garlic on paper towels.

3. Toss together beans and 2 tablespoons of the reserved garlic oil in a bowl. Transfer mixture to a serving dish; sprinkle with toasted garlic. (Leftover oil may be stored in an airtight container in refrigerator up to 1 week.)

Caramelized Pearl Onions

This is an uncommon side dish that is full of sweetness and buttery richness. Draining and patting the onions thoroughly dry helps them to caramelize. A bit of vinegar brightens and heightens all the wonderful flavors here. This is an ideal side dish for a grilled steak or roast.

SERVES **6**   ACTIVE **15 MIN.**   TOTAL **15 MIN.**

2 Tbsp. salted butter, divided
2 (14.4-oz.) pkg. frozen pearl onions, thawed, drained, and patted dry
1 Tbsp. granulated sugar
2 tsp. chopped fresh thyme
¹/₂ tsp. kosher salt
¹/₄ tsp. black pepper
2 tsp. white balsamic vinegar

Melt 1 tablespoon of the butter in a nonstick skillet over medium-high. Add onions and sugar; cook, stirring often, until onions turn golden brown, 8 to 10 minutes. Stir in thyme, salt, and pepper; cook, stirring often, 2 minutes. Remove from heat. Stir in balsamic vinegar and remaining 1 tablespoon butter.

Gingered Broccoli Rabe

Broccoli rabe is an Italian favorite that has a pleasing pungency that stands up well to bold flavors like the ginger and sesame oil here. The seeds of this vegetable are pressed to make canola oil.

SERVES **6**   ACTIVE **15 MIN.**   TOTAL **20 MIN.**

8 cups tap water
2 lb. fresh broccoli rabe, trimmed
2 tsp. kosher salt, divided
1 Tbsp. olive oil
2 tsp. minced fresh ginger (from 1 [2-in.] piece)
1/4 tsp. crushed red pepper
1 tsp. toasted sesame oil
1 Tbsp. toasted sesame seeds

1. Bring tap water to a boil in a large pot over medium-high. Add broccoli rabe and 1 teaspoon of the salt; cook until tender-crisp, 5 to 6 minutes. Drain; plunge broccoli rabe into a bowl filled with ice water. Drain well; coarsely chop.

2. Heat olive oil in a large skillet over medium. Add ginger; cook, stirring constantly, 1 minute. Stir in broccoli rabe, pepper, and remaining salt; cook, stirring often, until heated through, about 3 minutes. Stir in sesame oil. Transfer mixture to a serving plate; sprinkle with sesame seeds.

Ingredients 101

Winter squash have hard shells and thick flesh that require longer cooking than for summer squash. Common winter squash varieties include these.

Acorn: About 6 inches in diameter, this acorn-shaped squash has dark green ribbed skin and orange flesh. It can be halved, stuffed, and baked.

Butternut: Large and long with a round bulb at one end, this squash has beige skin and orange flesh and is great for baking and pureeing.

Hubbard: This irregularly-shaped gray-green squash with bumpy skin and yellow flesh can be pureed and baked into pies.

Spaghetti: Football-sized with creamy yellow skin, this squash is usually baked whole. The cooked flesh forms long, thin strands that can be served like spaghetti.

Turban: This squash gets its name from its distinctive topknot. Its shell is streaked orange, yellow, and green. It can be baked, steamed, or simmered.

Roasted Acorn Squash with Browned Butter

A touch of white balsamic vinegar boosts the sweetness of this buttery winter squash.

SERVES **8**   ACTIVE **20 MIN.**   TOTAL **45 MIN.**

Cooking spray
3 (1-lb.) acorn squash
3 Tbsp. extra-virgin olive oil
1 1/2 tsp. kosher salt
1/2 tsp. black pepper
1/2 cup (4 oz.) unsalted butter
1 tsp. white balsamic vinegar
2 Tbsp. chopped fresh flat-leaf parsley

1. Preheat oven to 400°F. Line 2 baking sheets with aluminum foil, and coat with cooking spray; set aside. Cut each squash in half lengthwise; remove and discard seeds. Trim and discard ends. Cut each half into 1-inch-thick wedges.

2. Toss together squash, oil, salt, and pepper in a large bowl. Spread mixture evenly over prepared baking sheets. Bake in preheated oven until squash is browned and tender, 35 to 40 minutes, rotating baking sheets between top and bottom racks and flipping squash after 20 minutes.

3. Meanwhile, cook butter in a small heavy saucepan over medium-low, stirring constantly, until butter begins to turn golden brown, 6 to 8 minutes. Immediately remove from heat, and pour into a small heatproof bowl. Stir in vinegar.

4. Drizzle butter mixture evenly over squash on baking sheets; sprinkle with parsley. Serve immediately.

Smoky Cheese-and-Nut Truffles

PREP & SERVE

The holidays are plenty busy without every occasion, meal, or dish requiring a heavy lift. The recipes on the pages 126 to 133 require minimal prep, simple assembly, and no cooking at all. Consider them our gift to busy hosts!

featuring

Smoky Cheese-and-Nut Truffles

Creamy Artichoke Dip

Emerald Ribbon Salad

Tricolore Salad

Smoked Salmon Buddha Bowls

Mascarpone-and-Amaretti Parfaits

Donut Hole Tree

Smoky Cheese-and-Nut Truffles

Flavorful conveniences like a log of tangy goat cheese, salty smoked almonds, fresh herbs, and citrus zest collide in a one-bite cocktail hour nibble guaranteed to get a swoon or two.

SERVES **18**   ACTIVE **25 MIN.**   TOTAL **45 MIN.**

1 (8-oz.) goat cheese log, softened
1 (8-oz.) pkg. cream cheese, softened
2 tsp. honey
½ tsp. orange zest (from 1 orange)
½ cup smoked almonds
1 tsp. minced fresh thyme

1. Beat together goat cheese, cream cheese, honey, and orange zest in a large bowl with an electric mixer on medium speed until smooth, about 2 minutes. Freeze 15 minutes.

2. Process nuts in a mini food processor until finely ground, about 20 seconds. Add thyme, and pulse until combined, about 3 to 4 times. Place nut mixture in a shallow dish.

3. Divide cheese mixture into 36 equal portions (about 2 teaspoons each), rolling to form 36 balls. Gently roll each cheese ball in nut mixture, coating well. Serve immediately, or cover and chill until ready to serve.

Creamy Artichoke Dip

Rosemary adds a woodsy backbone to this creamy artichoke dip that doesn't require baking. Be sure to mince your garlic before you add it to the food processor or it won't get broken down and incorporated into the dip.

MAKES **2½ CUPS**   ACTIVE **10 MIN.**   TOTAL **10 MIN.**

2 cups frozen artichoke hearts (from 1 [12-oz.] pkg.), thawed
1 cup ricotta cheese
4 oz. pecorino Romano cheese, grated (about 1 cup)
1 Tbsp. chopped fresh rosemary
1 tsp. table salt
½ tsp. lemon zest plus 1 tsp. fresh juice (from 1 lemon)
½ tsp. black pepper
1 small garlic clove, finely minced

Process all ingredients in a food processor until artichokes break into small pieces and mixture is well blended, about 10 seconds.

Emerald Ribbon Salad

There's enough acidity in this colorful salad to keep the apples from turning brown, even if it is made up to three hours ahead. Use a vegetable peeler to transform thick asparagus into thin ribbons, a technique that also works well with carrots.

SERVES **6**   ACTIVE **30 MIN.**   TOTAL **40 MIN.**

½ cup olive oil
¼ cup white balsamic vinegar
1 tsp. kosher salt
1 lb. fresh thick-stemmed asparagus
1 (10-oz.) pkg. angel hair cabbage
4 scallions, thinly sliced on an angle (about ½ cup)
1 large Granny Smith apple, cut into thin strips
1 (0.5-oz.) pkg. fresh mint, chopped

1. Whisk together oil, vinegar, and salt in a small bowl.

2. Snap off and discard tough ends of asparagus. Use a vegetable peeler to shave asparagus lengthwise into thin, ribbon-like strips.

3. Toss together asparagus ribbons, cabbage, scallions, apple, mint, and dressing in a large bowl. Cover and chill 10 minutes before serving.

Tricolore Salad

This is a beautiful and hearty winter salad. Bitter endive and radicchio have a sturdy texture that holds up well to the dressing. This comes together in a flash and is sophisticated and delicious with bright holiday colors.

SERVES **6**   ACTIVE **10 MIN.**   TOTAL **10 MIN.**

2 Tbsp. extra-virgin olive oil
2 Tbsp. red wine vinegar
2 Tbsp. minced shallots (from 1 shallot)
1 Tbsp. fresh lemon juice (from 1 lemon)
2 tsp. Dijon mustard
½ tsp. granulated sugar
½ tsp. table salt
¼ tsp. black pepper
2 cups torn Belgian endive (about 2 heads)
2 cups torn radicchio (about ½ head)
1 (5-oz.) pkg. fresh baby kale (about 8 cups loosely packed)

1. Whisk together olive oil, vinegar, shallots, lemon juice, mustard, sugar, salt, and pepper in a large bowl.

2. Add endive, radicchio, and kale; toss gently to coat. Serve immediately.

Smoked Salmon Buddha Bowls

If you need a fresh, healthy break from all the rich holiday fare, this recipe is for you. It is a light, bright, and simple composed salad with all the elements arranged individually in the bowl. This is best eaten soon after it is drizzled with the dressing.

SERVES **4**   ACTIVE **20 MIN.**   TOTAL **20 MIN.**

3 navel oranges

¹/₂ cup Asian sesame dressing (such as Annie's), divided

1 (16-oz.) pkg. shredded coleslaw mix

8 oz. sliced smoked salmon

¹/₂ cup toasted cashews

4 scallions, thinly sliced diagonally (about ¹/₂ cup)

Red pepper flakes

1. Peel and section oranges over a bowl; reserve sections. Squeeze membranes over a bowl to make 3 tablespoons juice; discard membranes. Whisk in ¼ cup of the sesame dressing. Add coleslaw mix; toss to coat.

2. Divide dressed coleslaw mix, salmon, cashews, scallions, and orange sections evenly among 4 shallow bowls. Drizzle remaining ¼ cup dressing evenly over servings.

Tasty Traditions

Fruit has long been a staple of holiday giving and holiday entertaining. Southern-grown citrus varieties not only make wonderful edible gifts, they are delicious for healthy snacking and for incorporating into your cooking, like in the Buddha Bowls above. Consider giving the gift of a citrus tree if the recipient has a green thumb and lives in the right zone.

Southern citrus grows in the LS (Lower South) / Zone 8, CS (Coastal South) / Zone 9, TS (Tropical South) / Zone 10, TS (Tropical South) / Zone 11.

Citrus plants of one variety or another are grown outdoors year-round in the Tropical South and mildest parts of the Coastal South. Most must be container-grown and brought indoors when temperatures dip below freezing even in the Lower South.

Varieties to give:

Lemons and limes: These are the most sensitive to freezes so are best-suited to the Tropical South.

Sweet oranges, grapefruit and most mandarins: These and their hybrids can endure a short cold snap or dip that hovers around 32°F and do well in both the Tropical South and Coastal South.

Kumquats, satsuma mandarins, and calamondins: These varieties are more resistant to cold and can withstand temperatures in the high teens, so they can survive cold snaps in the Lower South. Grow them in containers or cover trees to protect them during longer cold spells.

Hardy citrus: These varieties can be grown just above the citrus belt.

Mascarpone-and-Amaretti Parfaits

Mascarpone-and-Amaretti Parfaits

Whipped cream lightens rich mascarpone in the creamy layers in this elegant dessert parfait. Assemble these just before you plan to serve them so that the amaretti cookies remain crunchy.

SERVES **4**   ACTIVE **10 MIN.**   TOTAL **10 MIN.**

1 (8-oz.) container mascarpone cheese
1¹/₂ cups heavy cream, chilled, divided
4 oz. amaretti cookies (about 32 cookies), coarsely
    crushed, plus extra whole cookies
4 maraschino cherries (such as Luxardo), plus 4 Tbsp.
    syrup from jar, divided
Mint sprigs

1. Beat together mascarpone and 1 cup of the cream in a large bowl with an electric mixer on medium speed until whipped and combined, about 1 minute. Chill until ready to use.

2. Beat remaining ½ cup cream in a medium bowl with electric mixer on medium speed until medium peaks form, about 1 minute. Chill until ready to use.

3. Divide half of mascarpone cream among 4 glasses. Sprinkle each with ½ ounce crushed cookies (about 4 cookies). Top with remaining mascarpone cream and cookies. Top each parfait with a dollop of whipped cream, and drizzle with 1 tablespoon syrup. Garnish each with a cherry.

Donut Hole Tree

This donut hole tree is an easy riff on the fancy French croquembouche made from choux pastry puffs. This is so easy that you can get your kids and grandkids in on the action. We coated a Styrofoam cone with canned frosting that closely matched the color of the donut holes in order to camouflage the form. Then we used toothpicks to arrange the donuts in rings starting at the base. You can buy powdered sugar donuts, but we liked the snowy effect that a light dusting of powdered sugar gave the glazed donut holes. We tucked sugared cranberries and rosemary sprigs evenly into the tree for a decorated effect, but you could use peppermints, nonpareils, or even arrange decorated sugar cookies as an edible apron around the base of the tree.

SERVES **40**   ACTIVE **45 MIN.**   TOTAL **45 MIN.**

1 (12-in.-tall) foam cone
Aluminum foil
Canned buttercream frosting
80 toothpicks
80 glazed or powdered sugar donut holes
Powdered sugar, for dusting
Optional accents: sprinkles, rosemary sprigs, hard
    candies, decorated cookies, sugared berries

1. Cover foam cone with aluminum foil. Place covered cone, pointed end up, on a serving plate or cake stand. Coat with a thin layer of frosting to hide the foil.

2. Starting at bottom of cone, insert a toothpick ½ inch from bottom, leaving 1 inch of the toothpick sticking out. Press 1 donut hole onto end of toothpick. Continue inserting toothpicks horizontally and placing donut holes ¾ inch apart to create a ring around base of cone. Repeat process with remaining toothpicks and donut holes, working your way up cone until cone is completely covered.

3. Using a small wire-mesh strainer, sprinkle powdered sugar on top of and around entire tree. Decorate with accents as desired.

One-Pan Raspberry
French Toast

A PAN & A PLAN

Beautiful meals begin with a bit of planning and the right equipment for the job. From breakfasts to desserts, the pan is the key player in how these sweet and savory holiday recipes are formed, cooked, or served.

featuring

Marinara-Poached Eggs

One-Pan Raspberry French Toast

Broiled Salmon with Broccolini

Skillet Chicken Thighs with Green Grapes and
Pearl Onions

Green Chile Pork Stew

Dutch Oven Turkey Tetrazzini

Muffin-Tin Meatloaf

Muffin-Tin Quince-and-Pumpkin Stratas

Red Hot Apple Slab Pie

Marinara-Poached Eggs

This is a spin on shakshuka, a dish of eggs poached in tomato sauce that is served in the Mediterranean, Middle East, and North Africa. We used store-bought sauce for ease—and this one-skillet dish is all about ease! The runny yolks enrich the sauce, which is wonderful to sop up with toast or crusty bread.

SERVES **6** ACTIVE **20 MIN.** TOTAL **30 MIN.**

1 Tbsp. extra-virgin olive oil
1 1/2 cups chopped yellow onion (from 1 medium onion)
1 medium-size orange bell pepper, cut into 3/4-in. pieces (1 cup)
3 medium garlic cloves, thinly sliced
2 tsp. chopped fresh oregano, plus 1 Tbsp. fresh oregano leaves, divided
1 (24-oz.) jar marinara sauce
6 large eggs
1/4 tsp. kosher salt
1/4 tsp. black pepper
2 oz. feta cheese, crumbled (about 1/2 cup)
2 Tbsp. chopped fresh chives
Crusty bread

1. Preheat oven to 375°F. Heat oil in a large cast-iron skillet over medium. Add onion and bell pepper; cook, stirring occasionally, until lightly charred, about 7 minutes. Add garlic and chopped oregano; cook, stirring constantly, until fragrant, about 1 minute. Add marinara; let mixture come to a simmer.

2. Create 6 (2-inch) indentations in marinara mixture using the back of a spoon. Crack 1 egg into a small cup, and gently slip into an indentation. Repeat process with remaining eggs. Transfer skillet to preheated oven, and bake until egg whites are set but yolks are still soft, 10 to 12 minutes.

3. Remove skillet from oven. Sprinkle eggs evenly with salt and black pepper. Sprinkle entire mixture with feta, chives, and oregano leaves. Divide sauce and eggs evenly among 6 shallow bowls. Serve with crusty bread.

One-Pan Raspberry French Toast

Like raspberry strudel in French toast form, this is perfect as it is hot out of the oven, or you can gild the lily with a syrup drizzle and dollop of whipped cream.

SERVES **10** ACTIVE **20 MIN.**
TOTAL **9 HOURS, INCLUDING 8 HOURS CHILLING**

1 cup raspberry jam
1 (12-oz.) French bread loaf, cut into 1 1/2-in. cubes
Cooking spray
1 (8-oz.) pkg. cream cheese, cut into 1-in. cubes
4 large eggs
2 cups half-and-half
1 tsp. ground cinnamon
1 tsp. vanilla extract
1/2 cup packed light brown sugar
Pure maple syrup, whipped cream

1. Microwave jam in a small microwavable bowl on HIGH until melted and smooth, about 1 minute, stirring once halfway through cook time.

2. Place half of the bread cubes in a 13- x 9-inch baking dish lightly coated with cooking spray. Sprinkle evenly with cream cheese cubes; drizzle with melted jam. Sprinkle with remaining bread cubes.

3. Whisk together eggs, half-and-half, cinnamon, and vanilla in a bowl; pour over bread mixture. Sprinkle evenly with brown sugar. Cover tightly with aluminum foil; chill at least 8 hours or up to 24 hours.

4. Preheat oven to 325°F. Bake, covered, 25 minutes. Uncover; continue baking until bread is golden brown and mixture is set, about 20 minutes. Serve warm with maple syrup and whipped cream.

Marinara Poached Eggs

Broiled Salmon with Broccolini

This sheet pan supper comes together in a flash. Since it takes a bit more time to get a nice, smoky char, broil the Broccolini for a few minutes before adding the fish to the pan. The creamy side sauce is a cool complement to both the salmon and the vegetables. Substitute regular broccoli or asparagus spears here if you prefer.

SERVES **4**   ACTIVE **15 MIN.**   TOTAL **20 MIN.**

2 bunches fresh Broccolini (about 1 lb. total), trimmed
3 Tbsp. extra-virgin olive oil
1 ¼ tsp. kosher salt, divided
¾ tsp. black pepper, divided
4 (6-oz.) skinless salmon fillets
⅓ cup mayonnaise
⅓ cup plain whole-milk Greek yogurt
1 Tbsp. whole-grain mustard
2 tsp. chopped fresh chives
2 tsp. chopped fresh dill
2 tsp. chopped fresh flat-leaf parsley
1 tsp. lemon zest (from 1 lemon)

1. Preheat oven to broil with rack positioned 4 inches from heat source. Toss together Broccolini, oil, ½ teaspoon of the salt, and ¼ teaspoon of the pepper on a rimmed large baking sheet to coat Broccolini. Arrange Broccolini in a single layer. Broil in preheated oven until slightly softened and starting to char, about 3 minutes. Remove from oven.

2. Sprinkle salmon evenly with ½ teaspoon of the salt and ¼ teaspoon of the pepper. Arrange in a single layer around Broccolini on baking sheet. Return to oven, and broil until salmon is no longer translucent but still moist in center and Broccolini is charred, 3 to 4 minutes. Remove from oven.

3. Whisk together mayonnaise, yogurt, mustard, chives, dill, parsley, zest, and remaining ¼ teaspoon each salt and pepper in a small bowl. Serve alongside salmon and Broccolini.

Skillet Chicken Thighs with Green Grapes and Pearl Onions

The sweet-and-sour combo of the onions and grapes is sublime here. Use red grapes for less tartness. Steamed rice is the perfect side dish to sop up all the delicious pan juices.

SERVES **4**   ACTIVE **25 MIN.**   TOTAL **30 MIN.**

1 Tbsp. olive oil
1½ lb. boneless, skinless chicken thighs (about 6 thighs)
½ tsp. black pepper
¾ tsp. kosher salt, divided
1½ cups seedless green grapes
1½ cups peeled fresh red pearl onions
½ cup unsalted chicken stock
1½ Tbsp. red wine vinegar
1 Tbsp. chopped fresh tarragon
1½ tsp. unsalted butter

1. Heat oil in a large skillet over high. Sprinkle chicken evenly with pepper and ½ teaspoon of the salt. Add chicken to skillet; cook until browned on 1 side, 5 to 6 minutes. Remove from skillet.

2. Add grapes and onions to skillet; reduce heat to medium-high, and cook, stirring occasionally, until grapes begin to release their juices and skins are slightly charred, about 6 minutes. Return chicken, browned sides up, to skillet; add stock and vinegar. Let mixture come to a boil. Reduce heat to medium; simmer until a thermometer inserted in thickest portion of chicken registers 165°F, about 8 minutes.

3. Remove chicken from skillet. Add tarragon, butter, and remaining ¼ teaspoon salt to skillet; stir until butter melts and mixture is combined. Return chicken to skillet. Spoon sauce in skillet over chicken, and serve.

Green Chile Pork Stew

When you are exhausted, pinched for time, or simply tired of cooking, this is an ideal dump-and-stir recipe. Jarred salsa verde is a delicious shortcut to roasting, seeding, and chopping fresh green chiles. Plus, most brands have a tangy hit of lime, so you don't have to juice your own.

SERVES **8**   ACTIVE **20 MIN.**   TOTAL **20 MIN.**

1 (16-oz.) jar green chile salsa or salsa verde
1 lb. shredded smoked pork
1 (15-oz.) can pinto beans, drained and rinsed
1 (15-oz.) can fire-roasted diced tomatoes
2 cups lower-sodium chicken broth
1 tsp. ground cumin
Optional toppings: sliced or chopped avocado, sour cream, torn fresh cilantro

Cook salsa in a large saucepan over medium-high, stirring occasionally, for 2 minutes. Stir in pork, beans, tomatoes, broth, and cumin; let mixture come to a boil. Reduce heat to medium; simmer, stirring occasionally, until slightly thickened, about 10 minutes. Garnish with desired toppings, and serve immediately.

Green Chile Pork Stew

Dutch Oven Turkey Tetrazzini

Dutch Oven Turkey Tetrazzini

This is a classic recipe to use up leftover turkey but can be made just as easily with a shredded rotisserie chicken. This one-pot dish should be eaten hot from the oven as it gets gloppy as it sits. Enjoy with a crisp white wine and a side salad.

SERVES **6**   ACTIVE **30 MIN.**   TOTAL **30 MIN.**

3 Tbsp. unsalted butter
1 medium-size yellow onion, thinly sliced (1½ cups)
1 medium-size red bell pepper, chopped (about 1 cup)
1 (8-oz.) pkg. fresh button mushrooms, stemmed and quartered
½ cup (4 oz.) dry white wine
2 cups whole milk
1½ cups chicken broth
¾ tsp. kosher salt
½ tsp. black pepper
1 (9-oz.) pkg. refrigerated fresh fettuccine, cut into 3-in. lengths
3 cups chopped cooked turkey
4 oz. Parmesan cheese, shredded (about 1 cup)
Optional toppings: toasted sliced almonds, chopped fresh flat-leaf parsley, shredded Parmesan cheese

1. Melt butter in a Dutch oven over medium-high. Add onion, bell pepper, and mushrooms; cook, stirring often, until lightly browned, about 10 minutes. Add wine; cook, stirring occasionally, until most of the liquid has evaporated, about 2 minutes.

2. Stir in milk, broth, salt, and black pepper; let mixture come to a boil over medium-high, stirring often. Add pasta; cook, stirring often with tongs, until tender, about 4 minutes. Stir in turkey and cheese. Serve with desired toppings.

Tip

The following amounts should allow ample turkey for your holiday dinner, plus leftovers to enjoy later.

Type of Turkey	Serves
Whole (16 to 24 lbs.)	15 to 22 people
Whole (8 to 16 lbs.)	7 to 15 people
Bone-in Breast (4 to 8 lbs.)	4 to 6 people
Boneless Breast (2 to 4 lbs.)	2 to 4 people

Muffin-Tin Meatloaf

These oversized meatballs are slathered with the classic seasoned ketchup meatloaf glaze. Serve these with mashed potatoes and buttered peas for a pub-style supper.

SERVES **6**   ACTIVE **15 MIN.**   TOTAL **35 MIN.**

1½ lb. 90/10 lean ground beef
1 lb. ground pork
2 large eggs
1 cup Italian-seasoned breadcrumbs
2 oz. Parmesan cheese, grated (about ½ cup)
2 medium shallots, finely chopped (about ½ cup)
¼ cup tomato paste
4 medium garlic cloves, finely chopped (about 1½ Tbsp.)
1 tsp. kosher salt
1 tsp. black pepper
2 Tbsp. olive oil
1½ cups ketchup
1 tsp. smoked paprika
1 Tbsp. chopped fresh rosemary, divided

1. Preheat oven to 450°F. Using your hands, mix together beef, pork, eggs, breadcrumbs, Parmesan, shallots, tomato paste, garlic, salt, and pepper in a large bowl until well combined.

2. Brush a 12-cup muffin tray with oil. Gently shape meat mixture evenly into 12 balls; place each in a muffin cup. Bake in preheated oven until meatloaves are set but not browned, 12 to 13 minutes.

3. Meanwhile, stir together ketchup, paprika, and 1½ teaspoons of the rosemary in a small bowl.

4. Spoon ketchup mixture evenly over meatloaves in muffin tray. Return to oven; continue baking at 450°F until a thermometer inserted in thickest portion of meatloaves registers 160°F and ketchup glaze is set, 6 to 7 minutes. Let cool 5 minutes in tray. Sprinkle meatloaves evenly with remaining 1½ teaspoons rosemary.

Muffin-Tin Quince-and-Pumpkin Stratas

Reminiscent of bread pudding, these are welcome for dessert or as a fruity knife-and-fork breakfast treat. Pumpkin pie spice is a versatile blend to keep in your spice cabinet for sweet and savory cooking.

SERVES **12** ACTIVE **10 MIN.** TOTAL **45 MIN.**

Cooking spray
5 large eggs, lightly beaten
1 1/2 cups sour cream
1 cup canned pumpkin
1/3 cup packed light brown sugar
1 tsp. pumpkin pie spice
1/2 tsp. kosher salt
1 (1-lb.) French bread loaf, torn into 2-in. pieces
2 cups chopped peeled ripe quince or Asian pears
    (from about 2 large quince or Asian pears)
3/4 cup dried cranberries
2 Tbsp. powdered sugar

1. Preheat oven to 375°F. Coat a 12-cup muffin tray or 12 (2 1/2-inch) ramekins with cooking spray. Whisk together eggs, sour cream, pumpkin, brown sugar, pumpkin pie spice, and salt in a large bowl until smooth. Add bread; stir until liquid is absorbed. Fold in quince and cranberries. Spoon mixture evenly into prepared muffin cups; press lightly to remove air pockets. (Stratas will mound up as they bake.)

2. Bake in preheated oven until stratas are set and tops are lightly browned, 22 to 25 minutes. Cool in muffin tray on a wire rack for 10 minutes. Carefully run an offset spatula or butter knife around strata edges to loosen, and remove from tray. Arrange stratas on plates; sift powdered sugar evenly over tops.

Ingredients 101

Quinces are hard, round or pear-shaped fruit that look and taste like a cross between an apple and pear. The yellowish-white flesh is dry and tart, so much so that they aren't common in fruit bowls in the U.S., though they are very popular in Mediterranean countries. Find them from August through January in supermarkets. Quinces are often cooked in desserts, jams, jellies, and preserves.

Storage: Ripen quinces at room temperature and then refrigerate in plastic bags up to 2 weeks.

Red Hot Apple Slab Pie

Consider this candied apples in pie form. Red Hots candies melt with the heat of the oven to create a sweet-hot red sauce for the apples.

SERVES **15**   ACTIVE **30 MIN.**   TOTAL **2 HOURS, 30 MIN.**

CRUST

Cooking spray

2 cups (about 8 1/2 oz.) all-purpose flour, plus more for work surface

1 cup (8 oz.) unsalted butter, cut into small pieces

1/2 cup plain yellow cornmeal

1/2 cup (about 2 oz.) unsifted powdered sugar

3/4 tsp. kosher salt

FILLING

2 Tbsp. unsalted butter

3 lb. Honeycrisp apples, peeled and cut into 1/4-in.-thick slices

1/2 cup packed light brown sugar

1/2 cup red cinnamon candies (such as Red Hots)

1/2 tsp. kosher salt

3 Tbsp. cornstarch

3 Tbsp. fresh lemon juice (from 1 lemon)

STREUSEL

1 cup (about 4 1/4 oz.) all-purpose flour

2/3 cup packed light brown sugar

2/3 cup uncooked old-fashioned regular rolled oats

1/2 tsp. kosher salt

1/2 cup (4 oz.) unsalted butter, melted

1. Prepare the Crust: Coat a 15- x 10-inch jelly roll pan with cooking spray. Process flour, butter, cornmeal, powdered sugar, and salt in a food processor until combined and a ball of dough begins to form, 20 to 30 seconds. Pat dough into a 7- x 5-inch rectangle on a lightly floured work surface. Roll dough into a 16- x 11-inch rectangle. Transfer to prepared pan, letting dough come up edges. Chill at least 1 hour or up to 24 hours.

2. Prepare the Filling: Preheat oven to 375°F. Melt butter in a large skillet over medium. Add apples; cook, stirring occasionally, until apples just start to release juices, about 3 minutes. Add brown sugar, cinnamon candies, and salt; cook, stirring occasionally, until sugar and candies are melted, about 5 minutes. Stir together cornstarch and lemon juice in a small bowl; stir into apple mixture. Cook, stirring occasionally, until apple liquid has thickened and apples become tender, about 5 minutes. Transfer mixture to chilled Crust, spreading in an even layer. Bake in preheated oven 20 minutes.

3. Meanwhile, prepare the Streusel: Stir together flour, brown sugar, oats, and salt in a bowl; stir in butter until clumps begin to form.

4. Carefully remove pie from oven; sprinkle evenly with Streusel. Return pie to oven; bake at 375°F until topping is brown and juices are bubbling, about 20 minutes. Let pie cool slightly (about 20 minutes), or let cool completely (about 1 hour).

Glazed Chocolate
Sugar Cookies

BAKE & TAKE

'Tis the season for baking and giving. Pick something delicious from this inspired assortment of cookies, cakes, pies, and breads to whip up and enjoy at home, take to the office Christmas party, or box up to give to neighbors and friends.

featuring

Glazed Chocolate Sugar Cookies

Cherry Jammers

Best-Ever Chocolate Chip Cookies

Orange-Glazed Cranberry Christmas Wreath

Maple-Nut Brioche Buns

Bourbon-Apple Butter Hand Pies

Lemon-Poppyseed Mini Bundts with Elderflower Glaze

Coconut Cake with Coconut-Lemon Mousse Filling and
Coconut Cream Frosting

Honey-Quinoa Sandwich Bread

Savory Cheddar-Chive Sablés

Glazed Chocolate Sugar Cookies

Watch these cute cookies closely so they do not overbake.

MAKES **3 DOZEN**   ACTIVE **1 HOUR, 15 MIN.**
TOTAL **3 HOURS, 15 MIN.**

1 cup (8 oz.) salted butter, softened
1 cup granulated sugar
1 large egg
1 tsp. instant espresso granules
1½ tsp. vanilla extract, divided
2¼ cups (about 9⅝ oz.) all-purpose flour, plus more for
   work surface
¾ cup (about 2½ oz.) unsweetened cocoa
½ tsp. ground cinnamon
¼ tsp. table salt
1 (16-oz.) pkg. powdered sugar
6 Tbsp. water
Red and green food coloring paste (or desired colors)
Optional garnishes: candy sprinkles and sanding sugars

1. Preheat oven to 350°F. Line 3 baking sheets with parchment
paper. Beat butter and granulated sugar with a heavy-duty
stand mixer fitted with a paddle attachment on medium speed
until light and fluffy, about 2 minutes. Add egg, beating until
just combined. Stir together espresso granules and 1 teaspoon
of the vanilla in a small bowl; add to butter mixture, and beat
until just combined.

2. Stir together flour, cocoa, cinnamon, and salt in a bowl;
gradually add to butter mixture, beating on low speed until
just combined.

3. Divide dough in half; flatten each piece into a disk. Wrap
disks individually in plastic wrap; chill 30 minutes.

4. Unwrap 1 dough disk (keep other disk chilled until ready to
use); place on a lightly floured work surface, and roll to ¼-inch
thickness. Cut out shapes using assorted 3-inch holiday cookie
cutters, rerolling scraps once. Arrange cutouts 2 inches apart
on prepared baking sheets. Repeat process using remaining
dough disk (you will have about 36 cutouts total).

5. Bake in preheated oven in 3 batches until cookie edges are
lightly browned, 9 to 10 minutes. Let cool on baking sheets on
wire racks 5 minutes; transfer cookies to wire racks, and let
cool completely, about 30 minutes.

6. Stir together powdered sugar, water, and remaining
½ teaspoon vanilla in a large bowl. Divide glaze mixture evenly
among 3 bowls. Tint 2 of the glazes with desired amount of
food coloring; leave the remaining glaze white. Dip top sides
of cooled cookies into glaze. Arrange cookies, glazed sides up,
on wax paper. Decorate as desired using sprinkles and sanding
sugars. Let cookies stand until glaze is set, about 1 hour.

Cherry Jammers

*This dough needs to be slightly chilled to work with—if it's
too soft, pop it back in the fridge for a bit.*

MAKES **3 DOZEN TARTS**   ACTIVE **25 MIN.**
TOTAL **3 HOURS, 20 MIN.**

STREUSEL
6 Tbsp. all-purpose flour
2 Tbsp. granulated sugar
⅛ tsp. kosher salt
Pinch of ground nutmeg
3 Tbsp. cold salted butter, cut into small cubes

COOKIE DOUGH
1 cup (8 oz.) salted butter, softened
¾ cup granulated sugar
½ tsp. kosher salt
2 large egg yolks, at room temperature
2 tsp. vanilla extract
2½ cups (about 10⅝ oz.) all-purpose flour

ADDITIONAL INGREDIENTS
Cooking spray
¾ cup cherry jam or preserves

1. Prepare the Streusel: Whisk together flour, sugar, salt, and
nutmeg in a small bowl. Add butter cubes; mix together using
your fingers until mixture starts to hold together (there will still
be large clumps). Cover and chill at least 1 hour or up to 8 hours.

2. Prepare the Cookie Dough: Beat butter with a heavy-duty
stand mixer fitted with a paddle attachment on medium speed
until creamy, about 30 seconds. Gradually add sugar and salt,
beating until completely incorporated. Reduce speed to low;
add yolks, 1 at a time, beating until just incorporated. Beat
in vanilla. Gradually add flour, beating until just combined.
Gather dough into a ball using a rubber spatula. Place in a bowl;
cover and chill 30 minutes.

3. Preheat oven to 375°F. Lightly coat 1 (24-count) mini muffin
tray and 1 (12-count) mini muffin tray with cooking spray. Divide
dough evenly into 4 pieces. Divide each dough piece evenly into
9 small pieces, and shape into balls (you will have 36 balls total).
Arrange balls on a baking sheet; chill, uncovered, 15 minutes.

4. Press dough balls into and up sides of prepared muffin trays.
Spoon 1 teaspoon jam into each mini crust. Remove Streusel
from refrigerator; crumble into small pieces, and sprinkle
evenly over jam. Bake in preheated oven until tart edges are
golden brown and Streusel is lightly browned, about 15 minutes.
Let trays cool on wire racks 10 minutes. Remove tarts from
trays, and let cool completely on wire racks, about 45 minutes.

Cherry Jammers

MAPLE-NUT
BRIOCHE BUNS

MAPLE-NUT
BRIOCHE BUNS

Maple-Nut Brioche Buns

We guarantee that these sweet buns will outshine most any present under the tree.

SERVES **12** ACTIVE **45 MIN.** TOTAL **4 HOURS**

BUNS

¼ cup warm water (100°F to 110°F)

1 (¼-oz.) envelope active dry yeast

1 cup, plus 1 tsp. granulated sugar, divided

½ cup (4 oz.) salted butter, softened, plus ½ cup (4 oz.) very soft salted butter, divided

1 tsp. table salt

2 large eggs, lightly beaten

1 cup whole milk

1 Tbsp. fresh lemon juice (from 1 lemon)

¼ tsp. ground nutmeg

4 ¾ cups (about 20 ¼ oz.), plus ⅓ cup (about 1 ½ oz.), bread flour, divided, plus more as needed

Cooking spray

½ cup packed light brown sugar

1 tsp. ground cinnamon

GLAZE

3 Tbsp. salted butter

¼ cup packed light brown sugar

2 Tbsp. pure maple syrup

⅛ tsp. table salt

3 Tbsp. heavy cream

¾ cup coarsely chopped toasted pecans

1. Prepare the Buns: Stir together warm water, yeast, and 1 teaspoon of the granulated sugar in a small glass bowl; let stand 5 minutes.

2. Beat ½ cup softened butter with a heavy-duty stand mixer fitted with a paddle attachment on medium speed until creamy, about 30 seconds. Gradually add salt and ½ cup of the granulated sugar, beating on medium speed until light and fluffy, about 30 seconds. Add eggs, milk, and lemon juice, beating until combined, about 30 seconds. Beat in yeast mixture until combined.

3. Stir together nutmeg and 4 ½ cups of the flour in a bowl; gradually add to butter mixture, beating on low speed until well combined, 1 to 2 minutes.

4. Sprinkle about ¼ cup of the flour onto work surface. Turn out dough onto work surface, and knead until smooth and elastic, about 5 minutes, adding up to remaining ⅓ cup flour as needed to prevent dough from sticking to hands and surface. Place dough in a large bowl coated with cooking spray; turn to grease top. Cover with plastic wrap, and let rise in a warm, draft-free place until doubled in bulk, 1 ½ to 2 hours.

5. Punch down dough; turn out onto a lightly floured work surface. Roll into an 18- x 12-inch rectangle. Spread with ½ cup very soft butter, leaving a 1-inch border. Stir together brown sugar, cinnamon, and remaining ½ cup granulated sugar in a bowl; sprinkle over butter. Starting at a long side, roll up dough, jelly-roll style, into a log. Cut log evenly into 12 (about 1 ½-inch-thick) slices.

6. Place dough slices, cut sides facing up, in 2 (6-cup) jumbo muffin trays lined with king-size paper baking cups. Cover; let rise in a warm, draft-free place until doubled in bulk, about 1 hour. Meanwhile, preheat oven to 350°F.

7. Bake Buns in preheated oven until golden brown, about 20 minutes. Let cool in muffin trays on wire racks 10 minutes.

8. Meanwhile, prepare the Glaze: Melt butter in a small, heavy saucepan over medium. Whisk in brown sugar, maple syrup, and salt until combined. Whisk in cream; let mixture come to a boil, whisking constantly. Reduce heat to medium-low; simmer, whisking constantly, until glaze thickens slightly and becomes glossy, 3 to 4 minutes.

9. Immediately brush Glaze over warm Buns; sprinkle evenly with pecans. Remove Buns from muffin trays; let cool on a wire rack 20 minutes. Serve warm, or let cool completely, about 45 minutes.

Bourbon-Apple Butter Hand Pies

These are like a grown-up Pop-Tarts! Of course, kids can enjoy unglazed hand pies too (the alcohol burns off in the heat of the oven).

MAKES **1 1/2 DOZEN**   ACTIVE **30 MIN.**   TOTAL **1 HOUR, 20 MIN.**

2 (14.1-oz.) pkg. refrigerated piecrusts (such as Pillsbury)

All-purpose flour, for work surface

1 cup Apple Butter (recipe follows)

1 Tbsp. (1/2 oz.), plus 1 1/2 tsp. bourbon, divided

1 large egg, lightly beaten

1 cup (about 4 oz.) unsifted powdered sugar

1 Tbsp. whole milk

1. Preheat oven to 375°F. Roll out 1 of the piecrusts on a lightly floured work surface to a 12-inch circle. Using a 3-inch round cookie cutter, cut dough into 9 rounds. Set aside dough scraps. Repeat process using remaining 3 piecrusts (you will have 36 rounds total). Arrange 18 of the dough rounds evenly on 2 baking sheets lined with parchment paper; set aside remaining 18 rounds.

2. Reroll dough scraps; cut out 18 small (about 1/2-inch) rectangles (these will be the tops of hand pie "ornaments"). Poke out a small hole on 1 short side of each rectangle using a drinking straw. Set aside remaining dough scraps.

3. Stir together Apple Butter and 1 tablespoon of the bourbon in a small bowl; spoon about 1 tablespoon mixture onto each of the 18 dough rounds on baking sheets, leaving a 1/2-inch border around edges of dough. Brush dough edges evenly with some of the beaten egg; place prepared dough rectangles on top of each apple butter-topped dough round (with the poked holes facing upward). Top with remaining 18 dough rounds; press edges together using a fork to seal. (You will end up with 18 ornament-shaped hand pies total.)

4. If desired, cut out decorative shapes from any remaining dough scraps using a 1-inch cutter. Brush tops of hand pies with some of the beaten egg, and attach dough shapes. Lightly brush dough shapes with remaining beaten egg.

5. Bake in preheated oven in 2 batches until hand pies are golden brown, about 23 minutes. Transfer baking sheets to a wire rack; let cool 5 minutes. Transfer hand pies directly to wire rack; let cool 20 minutes.

6. Stir together powdered sugar, milk, and remaining 1 1/2 teaspoons bourbon in a small bowl; brush over warm hand pies. Serve warm, or let cool completely, about 45 minutes.

Apple Butter

MAKES **ABOUT 3 1/2 CUPS**   ACTIVE **35 MIN.**   TOTAL **1 HOUR, 55 MIN.**

3 lb. crisp, sweet apples (such as Honeycrisp, Gala, or Braeburn), peeled and cored

1 cup apple cider

3/4 cup granulated sugar, divided

3/4 cup packed light brown sugar

1 tsp. ground cinnamon

1. Cut apples into 1-inch pieces. Place apples, apple cider, and 1/2 cup of the granulated sugar in a Dutch oven; bring to a rolling boil over high. Reduce heat to medium-high; cover (leaving lid slightly ajar) and boil until apples are tender and most of the liquid has evaporated, 15 to 20 minutes, stirring every 5 minutes.

2. Transfer cooked apples and cooking liquid to a blender. Secure lid on blender, and remove center piece to allow steam to escape. Place a clean towel over opening. Process until almost smooth, about 10 seconds.

3. Return blended apple mixture to Dutch oven; stir in brown sugar, cinnamon, and remaining ¼ cup granulated sugar. Bring to a boil over medium-high; reduce heat to low, and simmer, uncovered, stirring often, until thickened, about 15 minutes. (To test whether it's thick enough: Using a wooden spoon, draw a line through apple butter on bottom of Dutch oven. If the line holds for 5 seconds before the apple butter merges back together, it's finished cooking.)

4. Remove from heat. Let cool 45 minutes. Spoon into airtight container; seal and refrigerate up to 2 months, or freeze up to 6 months.

Lemon-Poppyseed Mini Bundts with Elderflower Glaze

It's fun to bake up these perfectly portioned cakes for entertaining or giving. Be sure to heavily spray the Bundt molds. Baking spray with flour added is ideal.

SERVES **10** ACTIVE **30 MIN.** TOTAL **2 HOURS, 20 MIN.**

¾ cup (6 oz.) salted butter, softened
1¼ cups granulated sugar
2 large eggs
1 Tbsp. lemon zest plus 2 Tbsp. fresh juice (from 1 large lemon)
1 tsp. vanilla extract
2½ cups (about 8⅜ oz.) bleached cake flour (such as Swans Down)
2 Tbsp. poppy seeds
1½ tsp. baking powder
½ tsp. baking soda
½ tsp. table salt
1 cup whole buttermilk
Baking spray with flour
2 cups (about 8 oz.) unsifted powdered sugar
4 tsp. (⅔ oz.) elderflower liqueur (such as St-Germain)
1 to 2 Tbsp. whole milk, as needed

1. Preheat oven to 350°F. Beat butter with a heavy-duty stand mixer fitted with a paddle attachment on medium speed until creamy, about 30 seconds. Gradually beat in granulated sugar until light and fluffy, 3 to 4 minutes. Add eggs, 1 at a time, beating until just combined. Beat in lemon zest, lemon juice, and vanilla until combined.

2. Whisk together flour, poppy seeds, baking powder, baking soda, and salt in a bowl. Add flour mixture to butter mixture alternately with buttermilk, beginning and ending with flour mixture, beating on medium-low speed until just combined after each addition.

3. Generously coat 2 (6-count) mini Bundt trays with baking spray. Spoon batter evenly into prepared molds (about two-thirds full each). Bake in preheated oven until cakes are browned and a wooden pick inserted in centers comes out clean, 22 to 24 minutes. Let cool in trays on a wire rack 10 minutes. Invert cakes onto wire racks; let cool completely, about 1 hour.

4. Stir together powdered sugar, elderflower liqueur, and 1 tablespoon milk in a small bowl, adding additional milk, 1 teaspoon at a time, as needed to reach drizzling consistency. Drizzle over cooled Bundt cakes, and let stand until glaze is firm, about 30 minutes.

Coconut Cake with Coconut-Lemon Curd Mousse Filling and Coconut Cream Frosting

For this decadent cake, be sure you prepare the Coconut-Lemon Curd Mousse Filling ahead of time and make sure it is well chilled.

SERVES **12**   ACTIVE **50 MIN.**   TOTAL **9 HOURS, 50 MIN.**

Coconut Cake

MAKES **1 (8-INCH, 4-LAYER) CAKE**   ACTIVE **20 MIN.**   TOTAL **1 HOUR, 10 MIN.**

Vegetable shortening
1¼ cups (10 oz.) salted butter, softened
2½ cups granulated sugar
7 large egg whites, at room temperature
3½ cups (about 13 oz.) bleached cake flour
4 tsp. baking powder
½ tsp. table salt
1 cup well-shaken and stirred canned coconut milk

1 tsp. vanilla extract
½ tsp. coconut extract
Coconut-Lemon Curd Mousse Filling (recipe follows)
Coconut Cream Frosting (recipe follows)
Toasted coconut shavings, lemon slices, white chocolate shavings, and rosemary sprigs

1. Preheat oven to 350°F. Grease 4 (8-inch) round cake pans with shortening; flour pans. Beat softened butter in bowl of a heavy-duty electric stand mixer on medium speed until creamy; gradually add sugar, and beat until light and fluffy, 3 to 5 minutes. Gradually add egg whites, one-third at a time, beating well after each addition.

2. Sift together cake flour, baking powder, and salt into a bowl; gradually add to butter mixture alternately with coconut milk, beginning and ending with flour mixture. Stir in vanilla and coconut extract. Divide batter evenly among prepared pans.

3. Bake in preheated oven until a wooden pick inserted in centers comes out clean, 18 to 22 minutes. Cool in pans on wire racks 10 minutes; remove from pans to wire racks, and cool completely, about 30 minutes. Place 1 cake layer on a serving plate; spread about 1½ cups chilled Coconut-Lemon Curd Mousse Filling on top. Repeat with next 2 layers; top with fourth cake layer. Chill cake 8 hours or overnight. Spread Coconut Cream Frosting on top and sides of chilled cake. Garnish with toasted coconut shavings. Store any leftover cake, covered, in refrigerator (take out 30 minutes before serving).

Coconut-Lemon Curd Mousse Filling

MAKES **ABOUT 4 CUPS**   ACTIVE **20 MIN.**   TOTAL **7 HOURS, 20 MIN.**

½ cup granulated sugar
2 tsp. lemon zest plus ½ cup fresh juice (from 1 large lemon)
2 large egg yolks
¼ cup salted butter, cubed

1 cup sweetened flaked coconut
1 (4-oz.) white chocolate bar, chopped
½ (8-oz.) pkg. cream cheese, softened
1 cup heavy cream

1. Bring sugar, lemon zest, and juice to a boil in a small heavy non-aluminum saucepan over medium-high. Remove from heat.

2. Lightly whisk yolks in a bowl; gradually whisk about one-fourth of lemon mixture into yolks. Add yolk mixture to saucepan, and cook over medium, whisking constantly until thickened, 10 to 12 minutes. Add butter, in 6 batches, whisking constantly until butter

continued

melts, and mixture is well blended after each addition. Remove from heat, and pour mixture through a wire-mesh strainer into a bowl. Place plastic wrap directly on warm curd (to prevent a film from forming), and let cool completely. Stir in coconut.

3. Microwave white chocolate in a small microwavable bowl on MEDIUM (50% power) until smooth, about 1 minute, stirring every 15 seconds.

4. Beat softened cream cheese in a large bowl with an electric mixer on medium speed until light and fluffy. Add melted chocolate, and beat until blended, stopping to scrape down sides. Add cooled lemon curd mixture, and beat until blended.

5. Beat heavy cream in a medium bowl with an electric mixer on high speed until soft peaks form. Gently fold into lemon mixture. Chill until ready to use.

Coconut Cream Frosting

MAKES **ABOUT 4 CUPS**   ACTIVE **10 MIN.**   TOTAL **10 MIN.**

1 (8-oz.) pkg. cream cheese, softened
2 Tbsp. fresh lemon juice (from 1 lemon)
²/₃ cup granulated sugar, divided
1¹/₂ cups heavy cream

1. Beat cream cheese, lemon juice, and ⅓ cup of the sugar in a large bowl with an electric mixer on medium-high speed until smooth.

2. Beat heavy cream in bowl of a heavy-duty stand electric mixer fitted with whisk attachment on medium speed until foamy; increase speed to medium-high, and slowly add remaining ⅓ cup sugar, beating until stiff peaks form. Fold half of cream mixture into cream cheese mixture until blended; fold in remaining cream mixture. Use immediately.

Ingredients 101

Coconuts have a hard outer shell that's hairy with three soft spots, sometimes referred to as eyes, on one end. Once the outer shell is broken open, the nut inside has a dark brown skin covering white, firm-textured coconut meat. Fresh coconuts are at their peak from October through December; canned, frozen, or packaged coconut is sold shredded, flaked, and grated in sweetened or unsweetened forms. Coconut cream, coconut milk, and coconut oil are also available.

Storage: Store whole coconuts up to 1 month. Store fresh coconut meat in the refrigerator 4 or 5 days, or freeze it up to 6 months. Unopened canned coconut can be kept at room temperature up to 18 months; if packaged in plastic bags, it will keep up to 6 months. After canned or packaged coconut is opened, refrigerate in an airtight container up to a week.

Honey-Quinoa Sandwich Bread

This makes one hearty loaf to give and one to enjoy now. Or, you may wrap a cooled loaf tightly and freeze up to 1 month to enjoy later. It makes yummy avocado toast.

SERVES **10**   ACTIVE **50 MIN.**   TOTAL **6 HOURS, 5 MIN.**

SPONGE
3 cups lukewarm water
2½ tsp. active dry yeast (from 2 [¼-oz.] envelopes)
1 Tbsp. honey
1 Tbsp. sorghum
4 cups (about 17 oz.) bread flour
BREAD
¼ cup canola oil
4 tsp. kosher salt
2 cups cooked quinoa, at room temperature
4¾ cups (about 17 oz.) bread flour, divided, plus
   more as needed
Cooking spray
1 large egg
2 Tbsp. water
2 Tbsp. sesame seeds

1. Prepare the Sponge: Stir together lukewarm water and yeast in a large bowl; stir until completely dissolved. Stir in honey and sorghum. Whisk in flour 1 cup at a time until completely combined; continue whisking mixture until completely smooth, about 2 minutes. Scrape down sides of bowl using a rubber spatula. Cover bowl with plastic wrap; let dough rise in a warm, draft-free spot until doubled in size and bubbly, about 1 hour.

2. Prepare the Bread: Uncover Sponge; add oil, and stir using a large spoon or rubber spatula until combined. Add salt; stir to combine. Fold in quinoa. Fold in 3 cups of the flour 1 cup at a time until combined.

3. Sprinkle a work surface with ½ cup of the flour. Turn out dough onto work surface. Knead dough, using a bench scraper to help fold dough over and keeping your hands well floured. Add ½ cup of the flour to work surface; continue kneading until flour has been incorporated. Continue kneading for about 10 minutes, gradually kneading in remaining ¾ cup flour, until dough is elastic and springs back when pressed with your finger (it will be dense and a little sticky). Shape dough into a ball. Spray a large bowl with cooking spray; place dough in bowl, and turn dough to coat. Cover bowl with plastic wrap. Let dough rise in a warm, draft-free spot until doubled in size, 45 minutes to 1 hour.

4. Uncover bowl; punch down dough. Re-cover with plastic wrap, and let rise again until doubled in size, 45 minutes to 1 hour.

5. Turn out dough onto a lightly floured work surface. Divide dough in half, and shape into 2 loaves. Place each loaf, seam side down, in a 9- x 5-inch loaf pan coated with cooking spray. Cover loaves with plastic wrap; let rise in a warm, draft-free spot until doubled in size, about 30 minutes. Meanwhile, preheat oven to 375°F.

6. Whisk together egg and water in a small bowl. Uncover bread loaves. Gently brush tops of loaves with egg mixture, and sprinkle evenly with sesame seeds. Using a very sharp knife, cut 2 or 3 (½-inch-deep) slashes across top of each loaf.

7. Bake loaves in preheated oven until golden brown, about 50 minutes, covering with aluminum foil after 45 minutes if needed to prevent overbrowning. Transfer loaves to a wire rack; let cool in pans 5 minutes. Remove loaves from pans, and let cool completely on wire racks, about 2 hours.

Savory Cheddar-Chive Sablés

These are crisp and cheesy. The pecans around the edges get nicely toasted as they bake. Enjoy them with a glass of wine or cup of tea.

SERVES **10**   ACTIVE **20 MIN.**
TOTAL **9 HOURS, 40 MIN., INCLUDING 8 HOURS, 30 MIN. CHILLING**

1 (8-oz.) block sharp Cheddar cheese, shredded
   (about 2 cups)
1 cup (8 oz.) salted butter, softened
2 Tbsp. minced fresh chives
¼ tsp. cayenne pepper
2 cups (about 8½ oz.) all-purpose flour
1 cup finely chopped pecans
Flaky sea salt

1. Beat cheese, butter, chives, and cayenne with a stand mixer fitted with a paddle attachment on medium speed until combined, about 1 minute. Gradually add flour, beating on low speed until combined, about 2 minutes. Divide dough in half; shape into 2 (9-inch-long) logs. Wrap each log in plastic wrap; chill 30 minutes.

2. Place pecans on a large plate or cutting board. Remove logs from plastic wrap, and roll evenly in pecans. Rewrap each log in plastic wrap; chill at least 8 hours or up to 2 days.

3. Preheat oven to 350°F. Cut logs into 24 (⅓-inch-thick) rounds; arrange on 2 baking sheets lined with parchment paper.

4. Bake in preheated oven in 2 batches until lightly browned, 13 to 15 minutes. Remove from oven; sprinkle lightly with sea salt. Transfer to wire racks; let cool completely, about 30 minutes.

Savory Cheddar-Chive Sablés

Honey-Quinoa Sandwich Bread

NEED IT? FIND IT!

We wish to thank the following vendors and artisans whose products were photographed for this book. Source information is accurate at the time of publication. Many items featured in this book are one of a kind or privately owned so not sourced.

Accent Decor

Alabama Sawyer

Allstate Floral

Arhaus

Be Home

BIDK Home

Blue Pheasant

Bromberg's

Claire Cormany Art

Creative Co-Op

CVS Pharmacy

D. Stevens

Dillard's

Etsy.com

Europe 2 You

Farmhouse Pottery

Felt + Fat

The Fresh Market

Global Views

Hobby Lobby

HomArt

HomeGoods

Kelly O'Neal Artist

Leaf & Petal

Lowe's

Michaels Stores

Mud Australia

Paper Source

Pottery Barn

Table Matters

Target

T.J. Maxx

Walmart

Wayfair

West Elm

Zodax

Thanks to these contributors

We appreciate the contributions of these local businesses

A'mano

Alabama Sawyer

Bromberg's

Davis Wholesale Florist

Leaf & Petal

Oak Street Garden Shop

Thanks to the following homeowners

The Anderson Family

The Cobbs Family

The Gustin Family

The Lyons Family

The Hargett-Miller Family

Stock Image Photo Credits

Dan Reynolds Photography (Getty Images), p. 8–9 and 167 ; Lucas Allen, p. 48–49; Peter Frank Edwards, p. 60–61; Wilson Yu Photography (Getty Images), p. 70–71; Roger Foley, p. 82–83; James Zhen Yu (Getty Images), p 94–95

Pantry List

Grocery List

Holiday Memories

Hold on to priceless Christmas memories forever with handwritten
recollections of this season's magical moments.

Treasured Traditions

Keep track of your family's favorite holiday customs and pastimes on these lines.

Special Holiday Activities

What holiday events do you look forward to year after year? Write them down here.

Holiday Visits and Visitors

Keep a list of this year's holiday visitors.
Jot down friend and family news as well.

....

....

....

....

....

....

....

....

....

....

....

....

....

....

....

....

....

....

....

....

....

....

This Year's Favorite Recipes

Appetizers and Beverages ....

....

....

....

....

Entrées ....

....

....

....

Sides and Salads ....

....

....

....

Cookies and Candies ....

....

....

....

Desserts ....

....

....

....

Looking Ahead

Holiday Wrap-up
Use this checklist to record thank-you notes sent for holiday gifts and hospitality.

NAME	GIFT AND/OR EVENT	NOTE SENT
		☐
		☐
		☐
		☐
		☐
		☐
		☐
		☐
		☐
		☐
		☐
		☐
		☐

Notes for Next Year
Write down your ideas for Christmas 2021 on the lines below.